The Heart of the Matter

Rudolf Steiner (1861–1925), top left.
Elizabeth Vreede (1879–1943), bottom left.
George Adams (1894–1963), bottom right.

THE HEART OF
THE MATTER

Discovering the Laws
of Living Organisms

Olive Whicher

TEMPLE LODGE
London

Temple Lodge Publishing
51 Queen Caroline Street
London W6 9QL

Published by Temple Lodge 1997

A catalogue record for this book is available from the British Library

ISBN 0 904693 91 0

*The Publishers wish to acknowledge the support of this publication by the
Goethean Science Foundation*

Cover art: The Archangel Michaël (18th century), Collection Sekulic,
Belgrade
Cover design: S. Gulbekian

Typeset by DP Photosetting, Aylesbury, Bucks
Printed and bound in Great Britain by Cromwell Press Limited,
Broughton Gifford, Wiltshire

Contents

List of Illustrations

Foreword

As this century has passed, physics has increasingly had to renounce explanations based on straightforward models that can easily be pictured. No one model suffices to describe the behaviour of the atomic nucleus, for example. In a sense physics is in the vanguard of development here, as renouncing simple pictures is a big step away from metaphysical realism in which sense-perceptible models—scaled down suitably—are thought to explain the world. For example, the concept of the electron that has emerged is nothing like any object of direct experience. The price exacted by this is epitomized by the Copenhagen Interpretation of quantum physics: explanations of 'what happens and how' are not forthcoming from physics, only predictions of the outcomes of experiments in stochastic terms. We are left with an exquisite form empty of content. What, then, is matter? We do not really know! Biology tends to cling to picturable forms, such as the double helix of DNA because it works on a different scale. Paradoxically the very science that might be expected to lead us out of materialism has singularly failed to do so, while the 'hardest' science—physics—has gone much further. Our present consciousness cuts a 'slice' out of the whole, and needs to change if the greater picture is to come into focus. That is what this book is about.

Rudolf Steiner long ago pointed to the need for a different approach to science if these problems are to be surmounted. In particular the holistic perspectives given by projective geometry could be helpful, and more recent findings such as those associated with Bell's Theorem can be seen to point firmly in this direction. Steiner went further by describing another kind of space that is as much part of reality as our everyday one, and George Adams found an exact geometry for it, of polar-Euclidean form, which is often referred to as 'counterspace'. The possibility that other such spaces could have real significance should be no hurdle to scientists today in view of the exotic constructs entertained, e.g. in string theory. The fresh outlook to be won from working with counterspace has been described before, and this book is a further contribution by the author to making the idea accessible to a wider public. It is to be hoped that through this and similar books our way of thinking may change sufficiently to appreciate the pioneering work of George Adams (and, independently, of Louis Locher-Ernst).

N.C. Thomas
Chairman of the Anthroposophical Society in Great Britain

Introduction

The task of this book is to introduce in as elementary and pictorial a way as possible a fundamental mathematical approach to the laws of living forms and processes. We need to develop a way of thinking that does as much for the organic sciences as analytical thinking has done for technology in modern times.

George Adams, MA Cantab, to whom this book is dedicated, once wrote:

> Unhappily, modern geometry, like most of contemporary mathematics, is as a rule propounded in a highly abstract form, and therefore even mathematically gifted scholars do not ever find their way into the heart of the matter, where the significance of this geometry for their special tasks would dawn upon them.[1]

This statement is, alas, still true today. I therefore feel it justified to write as simply and pictorially as possible, as I did in the book *Sun Space*,[2] and also to include reference to Christology, which is indeed at the very heart of the matter.

George Adams, at Cambridge University during the First World War, was researching in physics and chemistry when his attention was drawn to that aspect of modern mathematics which was to form a basis for his life's work in the realm of science. He was a free thinker in regard to orthodox religion and was twice in prison for being a conscientious objector in that war.

Adams was convinced that the atomic theory is one-sided and leads to extremes. Several of his colleagues, notably Professors A.N. Whitehead and Bertrand Russell, saw that that aspect of mathematics which now goes by the name of modern projective synthetic geometry contains the forms of thought that serve the direction in which he was looking, and they drew his attention to it.

It was also during this time that the book *Occult Science* by Dr Rudolf Steiner came into his hands, the contents of which impressed him very deeply indeed. As soon as it was possible to travel again after the war, Adams lost no time in doing so, and put his question to Rudolf Steiner.[3]

His question was: Are the forms of thought expressed in this aspect of mathematics suited to the further development of the science of the 'ethereal formative forces' about which Steiner was speaking?

Rudolf Steiner's answer was immediately positive; and Adams had many opportunities of further conversation with him on the subject, between 1919 and Dr Steiner's death on 30 March 1925. George Adams's own death occurred on 30 March 1963, and it would be true to say that every day of those 38 years was devoted to the furtherance of Rudolf Steiner's work. Foremost among his closest associates were Dr Ita Wegman, leader of the Medical Section at the Goetheanum, and Dr Elizabeth Vreede, leader of the Mathematical-Astronomical Section, who greatly encouraged the writing of his major work *Strahlende Weltgestaltung*, published by the Goetheanum in 1933 and reprinted in 1965, under the direction of Dr Georg Unger, then leader of the Mathematical-Astronomical Section.

Steiner was saying that to understand the laws of living nature it is necessary to overcome the one-sided ideas which in the mathematical sense are only adequate when describing material forms and forces. In earth space, substances are either drawn downward towards the earth's gravitational centre or, as in an explosion, they are hurled outward and upward away from it.

He saw that although the processes taking place in the development of living forms do certainly have a spatial aspect, nevertheless the *causes* of these changing shapes are not to be understood in terms of mechanical and gravitational forces. He described what he called etheric or ethereal formative forces at work morphologically in ethereal space, which he also called counterspace.

Modern mathematicians, reckoning outward from a central point, say that space is determined as from a plane at infinity, which they call the 'Absolute' of Euclidean space. The Greeks at the time of Euclid or Archimedes never thought in this way, avoiding infinity in all their reasoning.

George Adams, and also Professor Louis Locher-Ernst, formulated mathematically the type of space which is polar opposite to Euclidean space. They saw that the Absolute of such a space must be an innermost point, which Adams called a 'functional inner infinitude'. Moreover, it is clear that such a space must be conceived tangentially and planewise, rather than centrically and pointwise. (See page 40.)

Mathematicians today are familiar with many different ideal conceptions of space but, interestingly enough, no one had thought it significant to formulate a polar-Euclidean type of space, which at first thought might appear simply to be as the mould is to the cast.

In the world of organisms, however, we learn from Rudolf Steiner that the substances of which the forms are created are *drawn upward*, under the influence of the ethers—the watery ether, the airy ether, the light ether and the warmth ether. These upward-drawing ethereal forces are all related to the sun and to the universe as a whole. They cannot be fully understood by means of the type of thinking which only sees and calculates the way substances sink down towards the gravitational centre or are hurled outward and upward in an explosion.

Rudolf Steiner describes these upward drawing forces using the word 'suctional' (*Saugkräfte*); and he describes the kind of space that accords with such phenomena as 'negative' (*Gegenraum*). We learn to create thoughts with which to envisage a 'negative' or 'counterspace', in which also the forces are anti-gravitational. The forces working to create living forms work in a way which is entirely opposite to the all too well-known gravitational and explosive forces.

The words *Leichte* and *Leichtigkeit*, coined by Rudolf Steiner to describe the upward-drawing, living forces of the organic world, are very expressive of a force more akin to the light of the sun than the darkness and weight of matter. Without an understanding of these living forces the world is dominated by materialism.

*

Today it has clearly become urgent to take seriously Rudolf Steiner's statements concerning the Christ, the 'Sun Being', who came to the earth at the 'Turning-point of Time'. He came as a physical human being, who walked on earth and died on the three dimensions of the Cross. He comes again in our time, into the realm of the life forces, but only to the extent that human minds become able to recognize Him.

In our time, the struggle between the light and the darkness is only too clear. In face of all that is happening, the approach made here to these timeless truths may seem abstract and difficult, but understanding lights up with every step taken and the light is evident among the present generations.

Chapter 1
Observing the Invisible

As time passes, a tiny seedling will develop into a fully grown plant—perhaps into a towering tree. Great masses of substance may rise upward, take on myriad shapes and forms—maybe exist in sunshine and rain, heat and cold—and remain alive for hundreds, even thousands of years.

Do we, in our modern scientific age, really understand the processes by which this comes to pass? Photosynthesis: what does this mean? We read: photosynthesis is the building up of starch and sugar in the green plant out of carbon dioxide and water with the help of the energy in sunlight.

What is the energy in sunlight, in comparison, for instance, with the energy provided by the gravitational force, holding huge masses of substance down on the surface of the earth?

The force of gravity is also not visibly perceptible, but we reckon with it daily and disregard it at our peril. It would, however, prove equally perilous were humanity to continue to misunderstand and disregard the true nature of the laws of the vital processes inherent in all aspects of life on the earth.

Science today explores the whole wide universe in terms of measure, number and weight, and it does this most efficiently. To compare what is done today, as a direct result of scientific research, with conditions only 60 or 70 years ago is quite astounding. Yet many aspects of life have greatly degenerated, and many species of animal and plant are becoming extinct.

While contributing enormously towards physical comfort and efficiency, modern science also kills; we all know how much is still at stake. What has not yet been fully realized is the potential, living power of human thought itself. Responsibility for the future of the human race lies with each individual human being today as never before. The more science teaches in purely materialistic terms, the harder it becomes to develop the life sciences, for example agriculture or medicine.

It is surely our task today to learn to understand the laws of living growth, just as through modern science we have learned to understand the use and even the creation of quite new substances. This task requires a renewal of the seedling forces of thinking, together with the awakening of powers of clear observation and pictorial imagination.

Rudolf Steiner's scientific insight into the laws of development in living processes was far in advance of his time as a result of his having worked to develop powers of spiritual insight, which he discovered within himself at an early age. In his autobiography[1] he described how, when very young, he realized that the things he saw with his senses were in space, but that there was also a kind of inner space—he describes it as a 'soul space'—which was for him a place of perception of spiritual beings and processes.

He describes how at school in his ninth year he discovered geometry, which filled him with enthusiasm. 'That one can develop, and let live purely in one's soul, pictures of forms, without impressions gained from external sense-perceptions, gave me the utmost satisfaction.' He saw that geometry provides a form of knowledge which appears to be created by the human being himself, although it has a significance quite independent of him.

> For weeks my soul was filled with the congruences and similarities of triangles, squares, polygons; I dug into my thinking concerning the question as to where parallel lines meet; I was bewitched by the theorem of Pythagoras.

The struggle for an independent understanding of truths experienced inwardly and at the same time outwardly is described in this autobiography—with repeated reference to various aspects of mathematics, which filled him with enthusiasm and gave him guidance. It was a strenuous young life, filled with practical experience on the one hand and with spiritual questions on the other. In his ninth year he realized that the local monks, with whom he sometimes spoke, must have important tasks about which he must learn. This, and his life between a free-thinking father and his own experiences as a choirboy in the local church, filled him with questions which made him feel very lonely.

Again and again, Rudolf Steiner formulates his auto-biography in mathematical thoughts.

I said to myself as a child, of course not clearly, but I felt: in the way geometry lives in one, so must one bear within oneself the knowledge of the spiritual world ... Here it is permitted to know something which only the soul itself, through its own forces, can experience. In this feeling I found it equally justified to speak of the spiritual world, which I experienced, as to speak of the sense-perceptible world.

Geometrical drawing was a favourite pursuit of this young student, who also realized early on that he must seek through the study of nature to come to terms with his inner spiritual experiences. He realized that it is only possible to come to terms with such experiences if thinking attains a quality which can reach into, and come to terms with, living manifestations. This was the goal he set himself.

Thus he built for himself a kind of Theory of Knowledge.

The life of thought gradually became for me the reflection shining into the physical human being of that which the soul experiences in the spiritual world. Thought-experience became for me actual existence in a world of reality, which is entirely unassailable by doubt.

This is not mystical experience. As surely as this young individual felt his feet firmly on the ground, and showed himself to be unusually practical and capable, so did he experience and begin to handle and train his own thinking. Maintained by his deep love for the world around him, he became a seer in the modern sense of the term—a spiritual *scientist*.

Although Steiner's anthroposophical movement has spread throughout the world since he died in 1925, the fact that his work is still not widely publicised is due on the one hand to opposing spiritual forces and on the other hand to the growing feeling that every person has a right to his personal opinions and must learn to think for himself and not just wait to be told. Steiner was a pioneer of such freedom of thought; he found a balance between science and religion and he called it spiritual science.

It is indeed possible, through individual and communal work, to learn to think clearly about the invisible forces which cause substance in living organisms to rise upward, visibly overcoming the force of gravity. This is a modern scientific task, and it is precisely a modern mathematical way of thinking that comes to our aid.

Is it really so far-fetched to conceive of forces that are anti-gravitational in nature, akin to the light rather than to the density of substance, forces that work peripherally rather than centrically? And would it not be natural to describe such forces as related to sun, moon and stars, rather than to the earth?

It is at the heart of the matter before us, with the continued help of Rudolf Steiner and the many scientist friends who have recognized his stature, to acquire more and more light on such vital questions as these.[2]

Such questions are indeed vital when a mechanically-minded and trained generation is involved in processes such as 'gene manipulation' and 'genetic engineering'. The words describe the one-sided mode of thinking underlying this aspect of modern scientific research, materialistic as it is, and open-ended. Where is it leading? Are 'building blocks' all there is?

Rudolf Steiner's scientific perception of the cosmic laws at work in the creation of living forms takes a far more balanced view. Just as a training in analytical thinking leads to the idea of an 'immune mechanism', so the kind of morphological studies to which modern projective synthetic geometry (morphology) leads gives access to a far more balanced and truer picture of the vital, living processes.

To understand the laws of the ethereal realm of formative forces in a modern scientific way requires an inner activity of thinking, through which a true balance may be found. It also requires a less one-sided reaction to the word 'spiritual'. This word need not have the one-sidedly ecclesiastical ring which it still has for many today.

In his medical book, *Fundamentals of Therapy*, in Chapter 3, entitled 'Phenomena of Life', Rudolf Steiner wrote, together with Dr Ita Wegman:

> Observation shows, after all, that the phenomena of life have an altogether different orientation from those that run their course within the lifeless realm. Of the latter we shall be able to say, they reveal that they are subject to forces radiating outward from the essence of material substance. These forces radiate from a 'relative' centre to the periphery. But in the phenomena of life, the material substance appears subject to forces working from without inwards— towards the relative centre. Passing on into the sphere of life, the substance must withdraw itself from the forces raying outward and subject itself to those that radiate inward.
>
> Now it is to the earth that every earthly substance, or earthly process, owes its forces of the kind that radiate outward. It has these forces in common with the earth. It is indeed only as a constituent of the earth-body that any substance has the nature which chemistry discovers in it. And when it comes to life, it must cease to be a mere portion of the earth; it leaves its community with the earth and is gathered up into the forces that ray inward to the earth from all sides—from beyond the earthly realm. Whenever we see a substance or process unfold in forms of life, we must conceive it to be withdrawing from the forces that work

upon it as from the centre of the earth, and entering the domain of other forces, which have, not a centre, but a periphery.[3]

Günther Wachsmuth was the first to follow up Rudolf Steiner's indications concerning the phenomena of life. In his book *Erde und Mensch* (Earth and Man),[4] he asks the question: 'What is life?' The book attempts to show that the earth is a living organism. It comprises a synthesis of various areas of research, particularly biology, meteorology and geophysics. By describing the dynamics and the rhythms of the earth as a whole, and in the organization of the forces in living nature, he shows that these relationships originate not in the substance but in the etheric organization of the living entity. Already, at the beginning of this century, Wachsmuth insisted that in the forms and processes of the living kingdoms of nature—such as assimilation and cell division, breathing and circulation, form and the form-creating process—the causes are not in the substance itself, but must be sought in the 'formative-forces organization' of plant, animal and human being. Wachsmuth uses the word *Bildekräfte*—'formative forces'—to describe the ether- or life-forces. He writes:

The body of formative forces in organisms follows a certain progression in the kingdoms of nature. The plant is in an intermediary stage between the mineral kingdom on the one hand and the animal and human kingdoms on the other, and it shows through this that it is far more open to influences from the surrounding world than are animals and human beings. Through its tropisms—heliotropism and geotropism—it gives itself up to the force-fields of earth and cosmos, whereas the animal and the human being, through the greater individualization of their formative-force bodies, have achieved a far greater emancipation.

Furthermore, the living expression of tropism has two aspects: spheres of activity in the surrounding world, which exercise particular influences, and the tendency of an organism, either as a whole or with certain of its members and organs, to open up or close itself off to such influences. In heliotropism, the plant turns towards the influence of the sun; in geotropism it turns towards the earth. For this the plant creates certain organs or spheres of influence in its own organism of formative forces, which are differently oriented towards those of the surrounding world.

Observe a germinating plant in the first stages of growth, and see how decidedly root and shoot progress in two opposite directions. The root grows in the direction of the force of gravity towards the centre of the earth, while the shoot actually overcomes this force of gravity and turns away from it; it strives upwards, away from the earth. To call such phenomena 'positive or negative geotropism' is really only a matter of words and no explanation. The puzzling thing about the being and functioning of the plant is that aspect of its organization which dominates over substance, orders the growth process in a polar way. At the root-pole the process strives towards the earth, at the shoot-pole away from it.

Thus, in developing Steiner's indications concerning the laws of the living world, Wachsmuth questions the sufficiency of the idea of 'positive and negative tropism' in the attempt to explain plant growth. Figure 1, taken from Wachsmuth's book *Erde und Mensch*, shows two cuttings from a willow, one hanging in the normal position of growth and the other hanging upside-down.

In both cases, the shoots have developed at what was originally the upper end (s) and the roots at what was originally the lower end (n). It is a remarkable phenomenon, showing clearly that it is simply in the nature of roots to grow downward and shoots to grow up. But how? And why?

The way of describing the process which the botanist calls 'geotropism' is clearly based on the idea of directions in earth space: up and down, above and below, inside and outside.

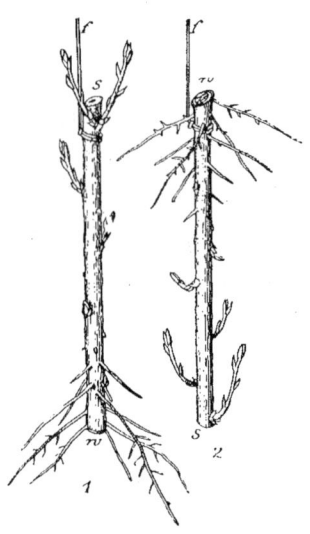

Fig. 1 *Positive and negative geotropism (from Wachsmuth,* Erde und Mensch*)*

These are all directions considered as from the midpoint of the earth. It is the space formally described by the mathematician, who thinks of three axes at right angles to one another and passing through a central point. One end of the vertical axis points to the north pole, the other end to the south pole.

This, the so-called Cartesian axial system, formulated by the famous scientist René Descartes (1596–1650), is the mathematical description of earth space—in which the plant roots grow downward and the shoots grow upward. We may ask: Is this the whole story?

The qualitative aspect of polarity in the plant

Already in that century, a close friend of Descartes, who is even now still little known, namely, Girard Desargues (1593–1662), began to formulate the ideas which in the 19th century culminated in modern projective synthetic geometry, which reveals a deeper understanding of space and of the polarity of plane and point.

On the basis of these ideas, the study of plant morphology reveals a further important fact in reference to plant growth. Whereas the root strives downward and spreads radially into the soil, the shoot, as it opens upward towards the light, takes on a quite different tendency of form, with a distinctly surface-like quality. While the core of the root becomes dense and hard, the heart of the shoot manifests as a hollow form, revealing less and less substance towards the interior. Think, for instance, of the heart of a lettuce.

It is not enough to describe the polarity of root and shoot simply according to the laws of earth space, formed around a point centre or an ordinary vertical axis. The arrangement of leaves and stems in the living world of plants speaks eloquently of quite other qualities and formative processes. This is true in all aspects of life.

Let us take a look at the forms of nature around us. Dead or mineralized matter is either compressed in hard lumps, even when crystalline, or it falls together and disintegrates into sand or dust. When life unfolds it reveals the delicate formation of surfaces, such as leaves and petals. In embryonic development the whole body becomes surrounded and interpenetrated by skins and epithelia, surface-like forms, that enfold again and again.

The plant reveals clearly the polar quality of forms in the contrast of root and shoot, as, for example, in the *beetroot* (Fig. 2) the expansion of substance in the root is very evident. The classical diagram from Sachs in Fig. 3 shows the side roots radiating from the central core and reaching pointwise into the soil. The leaves on the other hand grow from the peripheral cambium layer of the stem, revealing clearly the hollow space at the growing tip. Each leaf contains a bud, where the petiole joins the stem. This is the true picture of heliotropism and geotropism.

Fig. 2   *Root and shoot, beetroot*

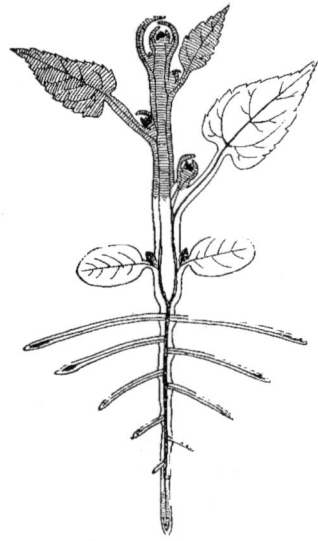

Fig. 3   *Morphology of root and shoot. (Diagram from Sachs)*

Leaves bedeck the earth. It is to these outspread leaf organs, in the last resort, that plants, animals and human beings owe their life on earth. Thanks to the greening of the plants, space transforms the breathed-out carbon dioxide into nourishing substances, renewing at the same time the life-giving oxygen in the surrounding air. Archetypal in the leaf is its outspread plane or surface.

The outspreading of the leaf into its surface clearly reveals one basic formative principle, while the rounded, condensed form of the root reveals an opposite tendency. Every leaf-surface is archetypally akin to the outspread surface of the heavenly periphery, while the root realm resembles the earthly process, typified by the idea of the gravitational centre of the earth. The capacity of the leaf to receive the cosmic forces of the light is proof of its kinship with the peripheral forces.

Contemplate, for example, an inner space such as is pictured so beautifully in Plate 1, a slightly magnified section, looking into the heart of a growing-point. Though clearly understandable in terms of three-dimensional space, it speaks also of another world, giving rise to the question as to what kind of forces are at work there. We know that in time this form will open out and become more and more visible in outer space. What are the forces at work there and how do they operate?

Exact observation and clear thinking leads to the idea of formative forces, which, rather than shooting outward, draw inward from the universal periphery. In polar contrast to the outward explosive aspect or the gravitational pull of the earth forces, which relate to localized centres, the ethereal formative forces exert an *upward-drawing force* and are related to the surrounding cosmos. The problem is that, while the former type of force is clearly sense-perceptible and accessible to analytical modes of thought, the life-sustaining forces are supersensible and have become lost to our modern-day thinking and perception.

The mode of thinking and imagining provided by modern projective synthetic geometry, and the ideas to which this mathematical field has given rise, provide a most fruitful way of educating thinking towards an understanding of the etheric world as described by Rudolf Steiner. A direct approach is thus provided towards an understanding in scientific terms of the forces at work wherever life processes reveal their forms. We become capable of observing the invisible.

The researches of George Adams, and of Louis Locher-Ernst and many others, show how fruitful it is for various areas in science to envisage these spaces, which are polar to the centric, Cartesian space of earth. Instead of being limited to the idea of points centred on a midpoint, as in the usual way of imagining a sphere, we are also able to imagine spaces formed of planes and surfaces—*planar spaces*—which have a relationship with the world periphery.

In order to come to terms with the laws of polarity expressed by the idea of a point space and a planar space, and to understand the way the polar opposite forces of these spaces play into one another, we must be prepared to practise drawing and to engage in active pictorial imagination based on these accurate drawings. Locher, bringing this idea of spatial polarity together with Goethe's idea of metamorphosis, once expressed the task as follows:

> Either one remains stuck with formalism, which after all does not lead to any ennoblement of life, or one decides to take experiences drawn from mathematical thinking so earnestly that they reveal their origin in a realm of absolute reality. However, in doing this we have to turn to the reality of the supersensible.[5]

Here we are concerned with a kind of understanding—a *knowing*—which must become *experience*. The faith and the hope that this is possible must never leave us; it is the achievement of the inner activity of a thinking individual which becomes essential. Of the three so-called graces—faith, hope and charity—the third, which means love, is all important. Here we come to the crux of the matter before us. To know truly is to love truly. Here lies the fertilizing power in all realms of life, including the search for knowledge through learning. In our search for understanding, we learn to transform cold intellectual thinking, however exact it may be, into warmth of understanding, not only in science but also in meeting the thinking of others. In thinking, which is a truly human and spiritual activity, we recognize the freedom of another human being and also our own freedom. In the hunger for knowledge, we may traverse different paths, but *freedom lies only in each individual's capacity for thinking*, and only here is it possible to distinguish right from wrong. The right development of science depends on a free and warm association of individuals, first of all in the realm of thinking.

So it is, indeed, that the new geometry—*morphology* is a better word for it—further developed by means of the idea of polar spaces and forces, leads towards an understanding of the supersensible. It provides a mathematical basis for research into the laws of the supersensible, etheric world. Through the fact that this research is based on mathematical principles, and not on fantasy of some kind, it stands as a science among other sciences. This accords with Rudolf Steiner's principles and with what he calls 'spiritual science'. Moreover, it accords also with his descriptions concerning the true nature of the sun.

To quote Edward Schuré: 'Quand la science saura, la réligion pourra'. When science reaches maturity of knowledge, religion will again have vital power. Science, which today is the recognized source of knowledge, together with a modern aspect of the art of mathematics, can renew our understanding of the true *religio*—reunion with the spiritual aspect of life. The word science means *to know*, but knowing has a threefold quality; the three become one in the union of science, art and religion.

Such ideas do perhaps go beyond our usual conception of science, but they do not go beyond the concepts of modern mathematics. Moreover, the basis is given for the interpretation of all types of force that overcome the force of gravity.

Buoyancy in water and the forces at work in the elements of light, air and warmth are all anti-gravitational. They have qualities which do not accord with the gravitational and explosive forces familiar to the physical sciences.

Contemplating the whole surface of the earth in the light of these thoughts, it becomes clear that this surface upon which we spend our lives, and which receives for us the necessary forces, is akin not so much to the dark forces within the earth but also to the light-filled spaces of the heavens. The surface of the earth is like a living organism, receptive to the ethereal forces of growth which originate in the heavenly periphery. And through the plant world, which belongs to it, the earthly surface is differentiated into myriads of individual surfaces— the green leaves which bedeck the earth.

In the rhythm of the seasons of the year the relationship varies between these polar forces that work upon the earth's surface, including also the regions layered one above the other: atmosphere, hydrosphere, lithosphere. There is not only an external, spatial, but a qualitative ebb and flow of forces. In winter the condensing forces of cold predominate; in summer it is the turn of the cosmic, peripheral forces to prevail, drawing forth what is akin to them. Water, which easily takes on the form of the sphere, incorporates both possibilities: the centric and the peripheral, the pointwise and the planar. When in winter the water freezes, the centric forces predominate; in summer it is the living forces of the universal periphery which call forth living forms.

Such are the scientific truths to which George Adams gave birth, as a result of the fertilizing power of the thoughts he received from Rudolf Steiner, together with the modern mathematical thoughts he met with in Cambridge University.

Chapter 2
Mobility and Polarity in Morphological Thinking

Perspective transformation

Let us now attempt in a simplified way to practise thinking in terms of mobile geometrical truths, leading to the understanding of mobile processes and interrelated spaces and forces, and taking into account outer and inner infinitudes.[1]

We walk the earth with equal steps, and when we work on it we measure it in miles or kilometres, yards, feet or inches, as the case may be. In all kinds of construction work finite measures dominate; they form the basis of practical life in three-dimensional space. This is Euclidean space. Even in the most modern achievements, such as exploring outer space or the tiny world of molecules, atoms, cells and nuclei, it is according to Euclidean space that the modern scientist and engineer thinks. (The astronaut takes his own little earth space with him when he walks out in his spacesuit on the moon!)

Modern projective geometry overcomes the limitations set by Euclid in his axioms and theorems; it frees thought and overcomes the rigidity of Euclidean spatial thoughts. From the 15th century onward, the mathematicians, together with the artists, developed the laws of perspective. First came the possibility of movement and then the idea of polarity.

This geometry comes to terms with the concept of the 'infinite', reaching the idea of infinitely distant points, lines, and a 'plane at infinity'. Also, innermost points at infinity become thinkable. A plane at infinity, containing lines and points, is a thought—just like any other plane. It is a plane beyond finite space but, nevertheless, it dominates the idea of three-dimensional space. The plane at infinity is called by the mathematicians the 'Absolute' of three-dimensional space.

In spite of the clear and exact way in which these concepts are reached, in accordance with the so-called 'axioms of incidence of point, line and plane', these thoughts remain surprisingly absent in the minds of many scientists and thinkers even today. It is partly due to the use of algebra that a pictorial way of thinking is absent.

In Fig. 4 the points Q' and Q'' are in a line parallel to two lines upon which a projective (perspective) process is performed. As all three lines are parallel they have a common point at infinity. This causes the result of the projective process to be in equal steps; we call it 'step measure' (arithmetical progression).

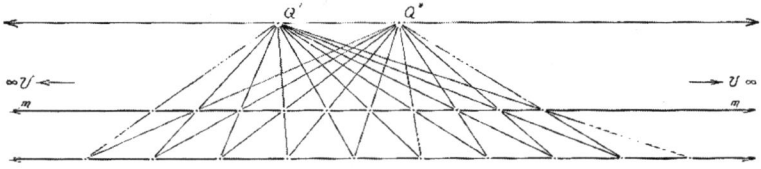

Fig. 4 *Step measure (arithmetical progression)*

In Fig. 5 the same projective construction creates a quite different measure. The reason is that movement has taken place; there is a change in the spatial relationships of the various active entities. The points Q' and Q'' are still projecting points from one line to another, but they are now both in the infinite. Moreover, the line m has moved and has a point in common with the line on which the projection is taking place; it now has the point O in common with that line. As we carry out the projective process with the lines and points in this changed relationship, we find another kind of measure appearing on the horizontal line. Whereas step measure (arithmetical progression) appeared in Fig. 4, it is geometrical progression which now arises, between O and a point at infinity (Fig. 5).

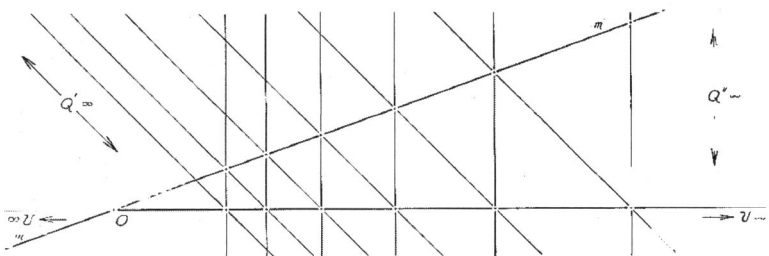

Fig. 5 *Growth measure (geometrical progression)*

Adams calls this measure 'growth measure', because it is the type of measure which is to be found in living forms. It comes about between *two* infinitudes—the point at infinity of the line and the point O, towards which the steps become smaller and smaller but which they will never reach. Here it is not that the steps retain a constant measure, but that they advance according to a constant *proportion*. We move from addition to multiplication. In growth measure it is the *proportion between consecutive steps* which is constant. This measure is poised between two infinitudes—that of outer space and an innermost point which functions as an infinitude within. This latter measure appears in Figs 5 and 7, and also in the linewise circles in Fig. 9(b).

A simple way in which to experience the difference between step measure, which is characteristic of the inorganic world, and a growth measure, which is revealed in organic forms, is to consider on the one hand forms side by side and on the other forms one inside another.

In Fig. 6 the quadrangles are side by side, as in Fig. 9(a). Projective geometry transforms this regularity into a picture reminiscent of perspective in art. It is, however, freer, for it is not necessary for one of the four points to lie at infinity and one in the centre of the vanishing line, as in a perspective drawing.

A harmonic law prevails between the four points on the distant line *and* among the quadrangles, which are set side by side. This creates a projective step measure, with the horizontal line functioning as an outer infinitude—a 'vanishing line'. It is a wonderfully harmonious experience to see the quadrangles emerging, one after another, with no resort to measurement. Choose any three points on the line quite freely and the fourth will arise with the creation of the first quadrangle!

Now set the quadrangles one within the other (Fig. 7) and the whole world will change. When the forms envelope one another the projective net will be spanned between *two* infinitudes, neither of which will be reached by the drawing. This is a projective growth measure. It is the type of measure belonging to all living forms. It is the principle of the Russian dolls—a toy much recommended by Rudolf Steiner for young children.

It is the line at infinity which is pictured by the Renaissance artists in what they call the 'vanishing line'; the plane of the earth is seen in the light of perspective. Hobbema's famous painting *Avenue at Middelharnis* (Plate 2) is a classic example. These artists descended, as it were, from the heights of the golden background and followed the laws towards which the mathematicians were leading.

Then came the further step; the idea of the inner infinitude is so wonderfully revealed again and again by Rembrandt, who lets shine forth the innermost light in the surrounding darkness. In his picture of the *Adoration of the Shepherds* (Plate 3) the man holding the lantern—an earthly light—forms part of the living circle surrounding the Child, who Himself lights up the circle. An ethereal space is formed in the darkness of earth, with the Child as the living focus of cosmic light in the heart of this warm inner space.[2]

Thus we see that from the idea of perspective transformation the artists also moved on to the idea of the innermost

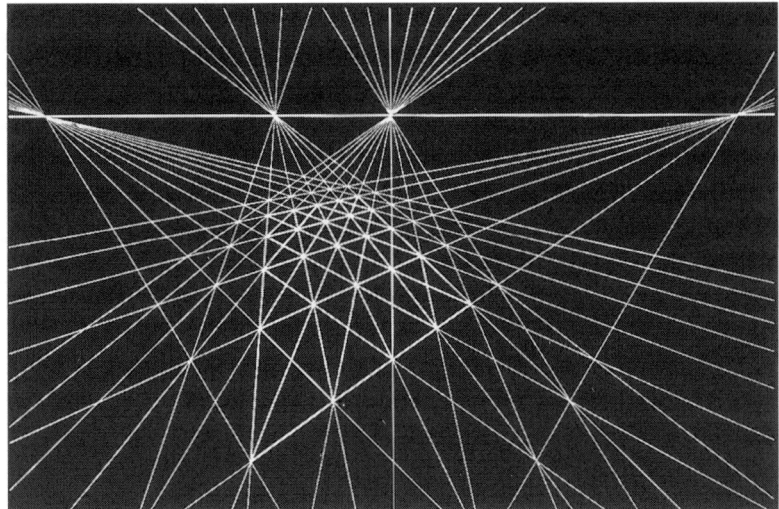

Fig. 6 *Harmonic net of forms side by side (step measure)*

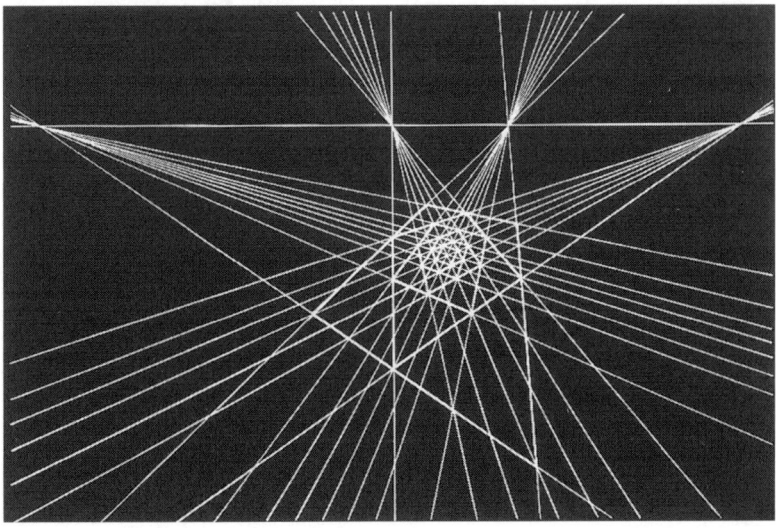

Fig. 7 *Harmonic net of forms one inside the other (growth measure)*

spaces; the art of mathematics went hand in hand with pictorial art.

The difference between the two circles in Fig. 8 is a simple illustration of the difference between the Euclidean and the polar Euclidean conception of a circle. The first is created of points, all equidistant from the central point, whereas the second is moulded from without by tangent lines, all of which are related to the line at infinity of the plane in which the circles lie.

Fig. 8 *Pointwise and linewise circles*

Perspective transformation and polar reciprocation are mathematical and at the same time morphological concepts, which are indispensable to the creation of a science of the organic worlds. The law of polar reciprocation leads directly to the perception of the idea of physical and ethereal spaces. George Adams formulated the laws of 'Polar Euclidean Space' and described the relationship of the laws proper to those two worlds—the inorganic and the organic.[3]

Polar reciprocation

Compare the families of circles pictured in Fig. 9. On the left (a), the circles are in the familiar step measure grid; they share a common point in the centre and also the line at infinity towards which—in thought—they might grow. On the right (b), the circles are in growth measure. They share both a line at infinity and also a point which—again in thought—functions as an innermost infinitude. In textbooks of projective geometry this point is sometimes called a 'star'.

The circles on the right have been drawn tangentially, thus emphasizing their peripheral quality and evoking the picture of a moulding process, as the circles move inward towards an inner infinitude in their midst.

The culminating theorem of projective geometry in the 19th century describes the law of polar reciprocation with respect to a circle. Bring the picture in Fig.10 into movement and see that if the polar lines move in their poles will move outward, and

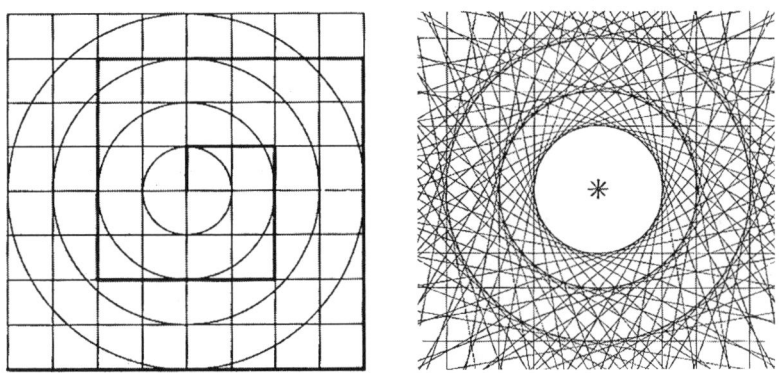

Fig. 9 *Families of circles*
(a) *Pointwise in step measure*　　**(b)** *Linewise in growth measure*

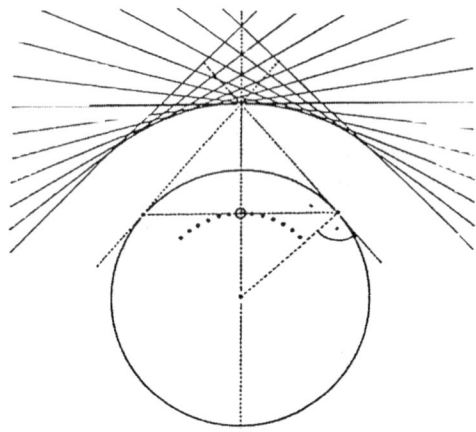

Fig. 10   *Pole and polar with respect to a circle*

there will be a meeting of tangent and point-of-contact on the circumference of the circle.

The forms of circle and sphere reveal two opposite qualities, concavity from within and convexity from outside. Euclid describes the circle as a manifold of points all equidistant from a fixed centre; his law of the tangent relates it to the centre by means of the right angle. Fig. 9(a) shows circles inserted in a step measure net of squares which emphasizes the fixity around a central point.

The family of circles on the right in Fig. 9(b) awakens a very different feeling. Drawn tangentially and related to one another in growth measure, they picture the kind of laws at work in living nature, as, for example, in a developing bud. The picture, true to a mathematical concept, is true also to the laws of the developing bud.

It is this planar experience of forms which Rudolf Steiner revealed and put into practice in art and his new style in architecture. Taking a piece of clay into our hands and moulding it into a sphere, we may experience directly this peripheral formative principle. The more accurately our hands approximate to the tangent planes at all points on the surface, the more accurate and beautiful the sphere will become. This is a most valuable educational experience.

The larger the sphere the greater its planar quality, whereas its form will be more and more curved and rounded as it becomes smaller until, ideally, it might dwindle to a mere speck of dust, a point in space. This leads to the idea of the disintegration of substance.

Analytical mathematics thinks its way into substance and reaches ideas such as atoms and molecules and ever smaller particles. It opens the way to extraordinary achievements, through the creation of machine tools and, indeed, machines of all kinds. It even looks into living processes and comes up with molecular biology and 'genetic engineering'.

Steiner called for methods that will show a balanced way forward, especially in medicine and agriculture. These steps in mathematics lead directly towards the understanding of the fundamental difference between a material point centre and the kind of centre revealed by plants and by all forms of life.

Polar reciprocation with respect to a sphere (or other spherical surface) is a valuable way of practising mobility and imagination in thinking, and it is an urgently necessary tool in the task of understanding the way living processes work.

Fig. 11   *Polarity with respect to a sphere*

Points are easy to imagine, but planes in modern geometry are not limited to any form or measurement—they are, indeed, limitless, and not so easy to imagine.

Think of the planar surfaces in Fig. 11; at first the plane touches the sphere tangentially. This is the typical relationship of the 'polar plane' with its 'pole'. If the plane moves, its pole will move, and vice versa; the movements are 'polar reciprocal', as in Fig. 11.

Figure 12 shows a sphere relating the plane above it with its pole within (construction as in Fig. 11 not drawn in). A chosen point on the plane is then related to the sphere by means of a number of tangent lines, which touch the sphere in a circle, thus determining the polar plane of the chosen point. (Each tangent line would also lie in a *plane* of the chosen point, determining a *planar* cone, which though impossible to draw can well be imagined.

Bring this picture into movement and learn to see that any

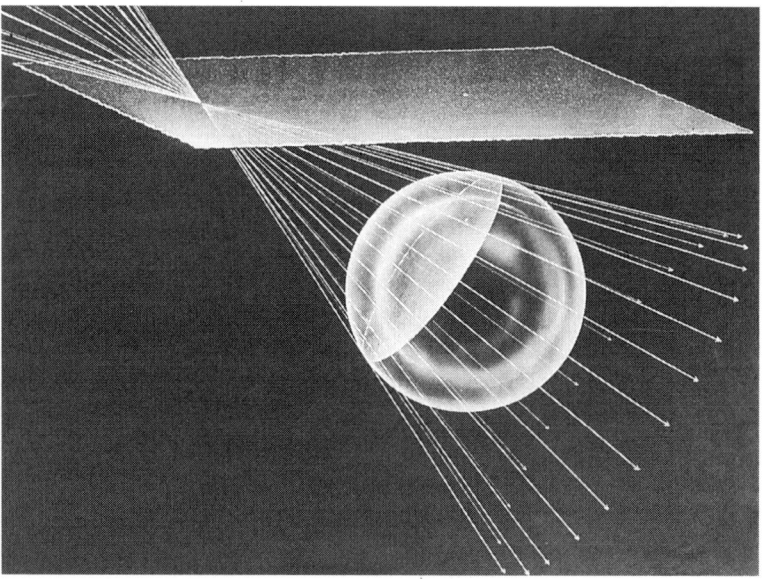

Fig. 12 *Polar reciprocation of points on a plane and planes in a point with respect to a sphere*

form drawn by the point in the horizontal plane will be reciprocated. A definite planar form would arise in the pole of this horizontal plane according to any movement of the chosen point. It is a demanding exercise in exact pictorial and mobile imagination, but well worth practising in a drawing.

The planar cones in Fig. 13 are all held in a point; it is the point of contact of the horizontal plane which is now tangent to the sphere. They are the planar forms polar to the family of circles, which are considered pointwise and drawn in a growth measure on the horizontal plane.

This gives rise to an innermost line at infinity within the planar, hollow cones; it functions like a line of innermost light in the heart of the 'cone space'. Mathematically speaking, the cones are in negative or ethereal space.

The ethereal cone space is manifest in the leafy growing-points of the myriads of plants growing on the earth's surface; it pictures the living processes taking place there in all

Fig. 13 *Family of cones in negative space. 'Spiritual staff'*

manner of shapes and forms. These are shapes into which the cosmic forces of life pour, to draw or 'suck' the living green substance upward and outward towards the light and warmth of the sun.

These are not mechanical forces and they are not to be thought of in terms of mechanical engineering. Nevertheless they are very real and without them there would be no life at all on the earth. Today much depends on human beings learning to think clearly and actively enough in order not only to understand these living forces but also to use them rightly, for instance in agriculture and in medicine.

Rudolf Steiner described the working of the etheric forces by using the word 'suction' (*Saugkraft*), perhaps for lack of a better word. The ethereal formative forces pour inward from the cosmic periphery, unlike the centric, gravitational or explosive forces. The formative forces come inwards towards the earth. In so doing these forces create living substance, for instance, in the growing-points of plants, drawing it upward and shaping it according to the surface-like qualities of water, air, light and warmth.

In Rudolf Steiner's words, the task is to recognize scientifically the ethereal formative forces of the universe, which lift substance as though from the mid-point of the earth and take it into the realm of those other forces 'which have, not a mid-point, but a periphery'.[4]

Such morphological studies leave no doubt as to the significance of polarity of the forms of root and shoot. Following the beginning made by Goethe as a scientist, Rudolf Steiner shows the way further.

George Adams first published the theory of Physical and Ethereal Spaces according to a mathematical formulation in 1933. Stated simply, we may describe it as follows:

Physical space is pointwise and centric. Its infinitude is an infinitely distant plane (the cosmic plane), which mathematicians call the 'Absolute' of physical metric in earth space. The measure typical of physical forms on earth is the repetition of equal steps, as in addition. We call this 'Step Measure'. It is manifest in an Archimedian screw and where forms appear side-by-side.

Ethereal space is planewise and peripheral. Its functional infinitude is an infinitely small innermost point. The mathematicians call it a 'star-point' and it forms the Absolute of this so-called negative or ethereal, formative space. The measure typical of living processes is in accordance with multiplication. We call this 'growth measure'. It is manifest in the logarithmic spiral, which appears in plants and other living forms, where the processes arise one within another.[5]

Wolfgang von Goethe (1749–1832) saw more in the living plant than can be seen from a mere study of its substances. Goethe saw in the young plant's stem an ethereal centre, which

Fig. 14 *Polarity in the developing shoot on a woody stem (from an old American botany book)*

he called the 'spiritual staff', and he recognized what he called 'metamorphosis', when the plant failed to achieve it. He saw plants growing in twisted and abnormal shapes and realized that when this happens the plant, having failed to metamorphose into flower and fruit, has also lost the capacity of seed formation.

A tree trunk reveals its kinship with the centric forms of the earth; yet in the new young growth, arising from the cambium layer under the bark, the young shoots can be compared to young plants, with their polarity of root and shoot, growing out of the ground as in Fig. 14.

George Adams described also in other books the ethereal, sunlike qualities of Goethe's 'spiritual staff', the innermost line of the stem, in terms of the cone space (Fig. 13). In our plant studies we have called this the 'verticon'.[6] Such new ideas stemming from modern geometry provide a scientific way of approach to the understanding of the upward-striving nature of plant shoots and stems in the field of ethereal forces.

The repeated appearance of the leaves in some plants is accompanied by a striking change in their shapes and may well be studied with the idea of perspective transformation in mind. When the flower appears, we see a dramatic change in forms and also in colour, which, with Goethe, we may call true metamorphosis. Here a new world is revealed, leading to the development of fruit and seed, and perhaps in time to an entirely new plant.

The rose is a beautiful example of the metamorphosis from leaf to flower. Calyx leaves are reminiscent of the leaves of the stem and they hold the balance between the sun space of the corolla and the moon space of the carpel. The light-filled space of the petals is there to serve the carpel, which, when fertilized, will itself become a sun space, and grow red and rounded to contain the swelling ovules.

Flowers are meeting places for winged insects of all kinds, especially the bees; they transfer the ripened pollen to other blossoms before the petals fade away, leaving a place for

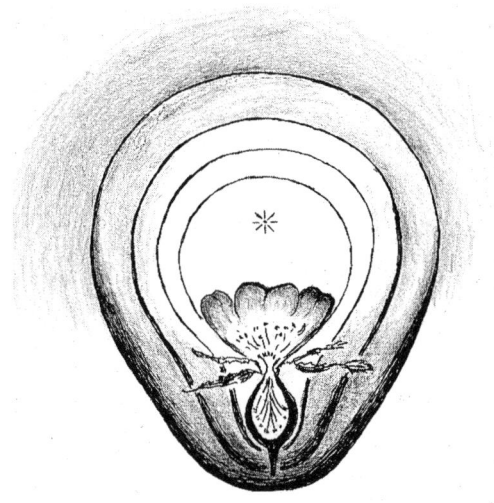

Fig. 15   *Polarity in a flower*

new life. The queen bee herself is fertilized by a drone in a nuptial flight high up above the earth. The whole flowering and ripening process belongs more to the sun than to the earth.

Rudolf Steiner, in his attempts to describe the polarity between the physical world and the spaces and forces of the spiritual world, very often used the lemniscate or figure-of-eight as a picture. Fig. 15 shows a transformed lemniscatory space with the Curves of Cassini, picturing the earth space below and the 'sun-star space' above. We have used these lemniscatory curves in the book *The Plant between Sun and Earth* to illustrate the conception of the sun-earth polarity in the plant.

The more we find our way towards the deeper understanding of what we call heliotropism, the more we shall overcome the one-sidedly materialistic aspects of present-day science. These metamorphic pictures of the plant—root, leaf and blossom—will help also towards the understanding of Rudolf Steiner's conception of the threefold human being. But first let us think more about the whole earth as a living organism.

Chapter 3
The Earth is a Living Organism

(What follows here is translated from George Adams in the first edition of *Die Pflanze in Raum und Gegenraum*, published in the original German by Verlag Freies Geistesleben, Stuttgart 1960, page 113.)[1]

We have in this idea of 'ethereal spaces' a way of thinking, accessible to science, which offers essential help in the attempt to recognize that the earth in its wholeness is a living organism. We think—perhaps as a first step—of the 'all-relating point'[2] of the ethereal space of the planet, coinciding with the mid-point of the earth. The earth forms its approximately spherical shape not only physically but also from the aspect of ethereal space. This means that we should attach great importance to what we may call the tangent plane of the earth at the point at which we inhabit it, that is to say, the approximately horizontal surface of the earth, in the region where we actually experience nature around us.

The place where we really experience the kingdoms of nature—and also ourselves as being belonging to nature—is, indeed, at the earth's surface, including the layers around and above it, which we call lithosphere, biosphere, hydrosphere, atmosphere and so on—concentric, spherical regions belonging to the organism of the earth. For the purely physical, spatial consciousness, it is the pointwise aspect of all this which is primary; this is what one instinctively considers to be real. The earth's surface consists, after all, of rocks, stones, grains of sand, particles of soil; even the hydrosphere and atmosphere, according to theoretical physics, consist of water and air molecules—and so on. Every stone, every grain of sand has its centre of gravity. Even one's own human experience of self, inasmuch as this relates to one's everyday concern with a point-centred orientation around a physical body, quite naturally emphasizes this aspect as pointing to a primal reality. Our very dwelling-place we seek out as a point on the map.

And yet it is the quality of *surface and plane*—particularly in the horizontal aspect—which surrounds and permeates us all the time, both as outer appearance and in inner, dynamic experience. We see it in every sea and lake; in every small, still surface of water; in many cloud-formations, and in the layers of mist over the early morning landscape. The orientation of our field of vision, thanks to our vertical posture, provides also a dynamic soul experience of this horizontal, planar world. Walking in the countryside and surveying the wide horizons, our field of vision sweeps over the horizontal tangent-plane, which belongs just as really to this place on the earth's surface as does the spot on which we stand. We live in this plane, which widens out to the horizon between earth and sky, just as much as in the force of gravity streaming through our vertical body. We feel ourselves inwardly carried and widened by the horizontal plane. Thanks to the steady firmness, which we owe to our upright stature—our overcoming of the gravitational force—we experience a feeling of unity with the rest of the world, of inner quiet and freedom. According to our individual destiny, this may be a more outer or a more potential dynamic inner experience.

The difference in the inner sense of life between people who live on a flat sea-coast, in the open landscape of a plain, or at the other extreme, in rugged, mountainous country, does not in the least depend on whether this horizontal plane of contact with the sphere of the earth-planet is an outer experience, which is of itself renewed with every glance into the surrounding world, or whether it is an inner dynamic achievement.

As an external, physical experience, the horizontal plane, be it a surface of water or any other planar niveau, such as may occur in wind-still air, is in the last resort the outcome of the centric, pointwise forces of gravity and of mass. One thinks of the force of gravity pulling at every particle of water and refers to an 'equipotential surface in the field of gravitational forces'. When, however, one takes seriously the idea of the 'ethereal Earth', the complementary aspect presents itself, when the horizontal planes are not just constructed composites made up of particles, but must be seen as whole surfaces, original in themselves. Just as every stone or every grain of sand, with its centre in mass, is a point-like member of the gravitational body of the earth, so the horizontal surfaces, which are again and again revealed in the elements of air and water, are peripheral entities, membered into the ethereal force-body of the planet.

In the ethereal space, with its 'Absolute' in the counter-spatial 'centre' and its planar quality, it is the force of levity (*Leichtekraft*) which works as a force of 'negative gravity'. According to its nature, the force of *Leichte*,[3] or levity, works in negative space through the fact that all the planar entities in such a space have an affinity for one-another—a force of attraction working between them, which is polar to the gravitational force of attraction, working between two mass-centres. We are helped to an understanding of the anti-gravitational quality of the living aspect of the planet by the further development of the ideas already reached in the 19th century in geometry.

There is an active field of upward movement, which balances out the gravitational forces at work in earth-substance. (The Archimedian force of buoyancy is explained in classical hydrostatics, not as an active, anti-gravitational force but rather as the resultant of a combination of forces in a situation that is either more or less under the influence of gravity.) Under some conditions, even physical entities are taken up into this anti-gravitational field. There are phenomena that cannot be explained on the basis of the interplay of pointwise—or atomistic—forces alone. We have an archetypal phenomenon before us in the upward growth and development of plants.

Moreover, in the seasonal changes of the anti-gravitational field of the planet earth, we must learn to recognize the processes deriving from the plane at infinity of our physical world-space, and see in it the region of origin of forces of balance—the central anti-gravitational plane (*Leichte-ebene*)[4] of our planet. Through the fact that at one and the same time the forces of the physical centre of the earth and those of the ethereal infinitude within—the all-relating point of the ethereal earth—are functioning together, we learn to understand the great doubly polar relationship between the world of matter and the worlds of spirit.

> The centre of gravity of the physical forces of the planet earth is at the same time the 'all-relating point' of the ethereal space of the planet.
>
> The plane of levity of the ethereal forces of the planet earth is at the same time the 'all-embracing plane' of the universal space of the planet.

In this statement consisting of pure thoughts lies the setting for the questions concerning nature from which we take our start. One might ask oneself whether this concentric relationship of the physical and ethereal planetary spaces—in other words, of the gravitational and levitational fields of the planet—is subject to local and above all seasonal variations. The phenomena of plant life point perhaps to a yearly swing to and fro of the middle plane, between the northern and southern hemipheres. The plane of levity (*Leichte-Ebene*) of the planet would accordingly approach from the infinite distances and come nearer the earth on the side which has summer, and then in a half-yearly course retreat through the infinite distance and swing to the opposite side of the earth. This would be the peripheral reflection or opposite picture to a pendulum movement in centric space, in which the balanced situation, instead of being in an inner position between the extremes of the pendulum swing, would be out in the world-periphery, which, according to our earthly measurements, we experience as being infinitely far away.

If then we take the circling and vortical movements of the earth into account, implied by the astronomical and meteorological phenomena, then far more organic, rhythmically seasonable movements are thinkable, in the ethereal body of the planet. They would be related to this pendulum swing in peripheral space as are the laws of the rhythmic movement of a top to a simple pendulum swing.

Through the fact that we are considering the earth to have not only a physical body but also an ethereal body, we have a quite new way of thinking about the phenomena. Stated in more mathematical terms: through the fact that we look at all events happening on the earth not only from a purely spatial planetary, cosmic aspect, our approach brings something quite new to science.

A play of forces, which is inexplicable in terms of purely physical (molecular) theories as long as the research is limited to the four walls of a laboratory, and taking into account only the surrounding relative emptiness of ordinary space, considered pointwise, will, from the aspect of ethereal space, be related to the whole earth-planet or at least to wide reaches of the earth's surface. This is particularly the case in all hydrodynamic and aerodynamic phenomena. Considered thus, the idea of the ethereal counterspace, with its peripheral play of forces, opens up new points of view also for meteorology.

The all-relating innermost point of the ethereal space of the whole planet earth, as described here in relation to the macrocosm, is to be seen everywhere on the earth in micro-cosmic form, where countless living organisms on the earth reveal it. Look into the heart of a developing shoot and see the 'cone space', with its innermost, all-relating line, or look into the heart of a flower, its hollow space, and see the logarithmic spirals, as, for instance, in the sunflower.

Everywhere, in plant, animal and human forms—even in the crystal forms of earth—the living formative forces of the etheric worlds are to be seen, provided we have developed the thoughts with which to perceive them.

This is what Rudolf Steiner was able to teach, once the question was put to him. The thoughts of modern math-ematics, which teach the laws of synthesis as well as analysis, are essential to this task. It becomes more and more evident at the end of the millennium that there is a confrontation between extreme forces, and that humanity is struggling to hold the balance.

This is only possible when science understands that the earth is a living organism—indeed, that the universe itself is living. The modern scientific task is to seek the laws of life at work in gene and galaxy alike. This will be achieved not by seeking to understand the universe and all that happens in it by means of mechanistic thoughts only, but also by learning to raise intellectual thinking towards the spiritual realms in which life does actually function.

The human being, unlike any other living forms on earth, is endowed with the powers of thinking, feeling and willing. Unique to the human being is the power of active thinking.

'Negative space' and 'ethereal forces'—practical research in laboratory and field

Rudolf Steiner, speaking of ethereal or 'negative' spaces in regard to the understanding of the laws of living processes, uses the idea of 'nothingness'—*ein Nichts*—and he brings together with this concept the word *chaos*. He sometimes uses this word in the way we usually think of it, but it is important to realize that this is not always so.

It is helpful not to think only of the two words *cosmos* and *chaos* as meaning order on the one hand and destruction on the other. The word used in its ancient sense—the Greek word *Xáos*—does not mean destruction. On the contrary, it describes a region empty of formed matter, but ready to receive new, living growth or development, such as is to be found in a seed or any germinating process. Look again at Plate 1.

The inward infinitude of a living process, such as the growing-point in the plant world, or the heart of a rose, is an example of the true meaning of the Greek word *Xáos*. This is what Rudolf Steiner is so often trying to call forth in our minds, which, in the one-sidedly physical and analytical way of thinking of today, meets with such opposition.

To picture clearly an ethereal space in thought requires precisely the overcoming of such opposition, which lies also deeply in our own thinking. The need to become true citizens of the earth has demanded at first the sacrifice of seeing beyond the earth in the visionary way, which was possible in the past. The time has, however, come in this century for the next step forward. *Thinking must become the clear pathway towards the spiritualizing of science.*

The growing-points in all aspects of living nature over the earth await the understanding of man today. Every germinating plant seed and budding shoot calls for such understanding, but so do the developing embryos of animals and human beings!

An embryo *is* actually such a receptive, ethereal space—a realm of 'empty nothingness' into which new formative processes can work, as they cannot do into the ready-made bricks and mortar of man-made forms. To know this as a scientific fact is surely a first step towards the healing of present-day juvenile crime—the result of a one-sided education.

The healing of the present-day troubles of teenagers and young adults rests not in a return to religion as it was in the past, but in the capacity to teach the facts of the organic sciences in a true way. The spiritualizing of science demands also the right approach to the cosmic truths of religion.

To understand the spiritual, creative processes at work in a developing embryo is to recognize that it is only when laid on the earthly support that the child is really on earth, and not before. It is a spiritual being, who descends from cosmic realms, through sun and moon spaces, into the three-dimensional space of earth.

Even then, however, we must learn equally clearly in modern scientific terms to understand this human being in his cosmic-earthly polarity. It is not just a physical form that lies there, understandable by means of materialistic, mechanical ways of thinking. There is more to it than meets the eye!

Thus our task is clearly expressed. Our eyes must be trained to see more than what appears visibly there before us. We must learn to observe in thought the invisible forces and powers which give rise to all living processes.

Just as mathematics through the ages has guided human thinking in the understanding of forms and formative processes, so it is today. Our time sets this task urgently before us.

One of the early pioneers of anthroposophical science was Dr Alexander Leroi, the medical doctor who founded the Hiscia Laboratory in Arlesheim, in connection with the Lukas Klinic, in order to put into practice Rudolf Steiner's indications towards the prevention and healing of cancer. Leroi was very aware of the work of Adams, who was also a member of the group who formed the experimental team. Anthroposophical medicine has since spread worldwide.

Steiner saw this illness as a phenomenon of our time, resulting from misconceptions concerning the intake of certain substances but also from the insufficient understanding of the true nature of the life forces. A weakening of the etheric formative forces results in the abnormal proliferation of cells in the physical body, thus causing cancerous and uncontrolled growth. In this connection, Rudolf Steiner turned to the mistletoe plant, which is an age-old remedial plant.

Mistletoe is a parasite on other plants. Without true roots, its suckers gain nourishment from the wood of various kinds of tree. It takes several years to grow into a beautiful spherical shape and bears white, transparent berries, which are eaten and then deposited on the trees by birds, through their digestive system, resulting in the germination of new plants.

Steiner proposed mixing the juice of berries picked from the plants in summer and berries picked in winter by means of a centrifuge, thus ensuring that the mixing process takes place away from the influence of the earthly forces of gravity.

The picture is of a plant which has little or no relation to the earth, and of a mixing process taking place as much as possible out of reach of the forces of the earth. All this is in order to heal a very physical, one might say quantitative, illness. Mistletoe berries, together with leaves and stems, are taken from different species of tree, to deal with cancerous growths in the various parts of the body.

It was the destiny of Alexander Leroi himself to die of cancer in the early stages of the development of the Lukas Klinik in Arlesheim, work which was continued and developed by his wife, Dr Rita Leroi, until her own death in 1987.

In his later years, George Adams, always urgently aware of Dr Steiner's insistence on the need to understand the planar, anti-gravitational quality of the etheric processes, and always on the lookout for the necessary mathematical basis for such work, made a discovery in the British Museum Library. He found a little-known and long-forgotten realm of mathematical research from around the turn of this century. It is work done by Sophus Lie and Felix Klein on curves of a higher order than circles and their projective transformations, or even of the lemniscate and Curves of Cassini.

The lemniscate is a pointwise curve; it cannot be created in such a way that, for instance, one loop may be created by means of tangent lines. This, and the Curves of Cassini, were used by Steiner to describe morphological and qualitative polarity. But Adams was not satisfied with the picture it gives, and on this account kept searching for an alternative. He was overjoyed when he found the long-forgotten realm of mathematics which he called by the name of 'path curves and path-curve surfaces'. (See Fig. 16 and Plate 4.)

Only a very brief description of this work is possible here. Since Adams died in 1963, Lawrence Edwards, who collaborated with him during the last twelve years of his life, has taken the work further. He was the first to demonstrate by means of detailed measurement and advanced mathematical calculations and experimentation that surfaces in plant, animal and human forms reveal the same type of morphological quality as those attainable in this new field of mathematics.[5]

Such surfaces are the very essence of living forms, to be seen in the shapes of buds, of eggs and of vortices. They appear in

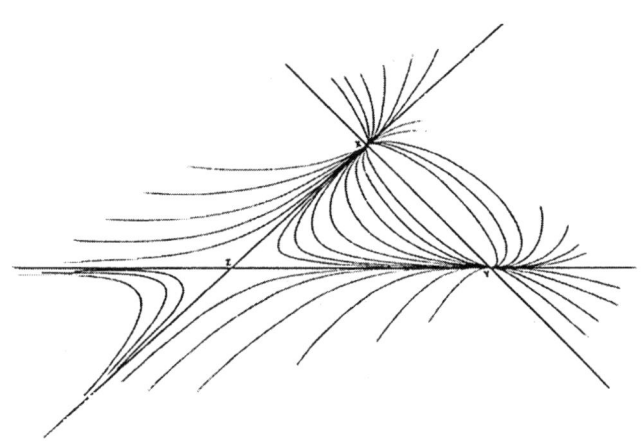

Fig. 16   *'Path curves' in the plane*

the moving elements of water, air and warmth, and they permeate the human body.These are the forms on earth into which the life-giving ethereal forces work. Even the water spiralling away down the plug-hole will be receiving the purifying and vitalizing forces of the elemental world through such formative processes.

More recently, Georg Sonder, who works in the firm Helixor (which also produces a remedy for cancer) and who visited Lawrence Edwards in order to learn to create path-curve surfaces, has been able to make a vessel according to these mathematical laws.[6]

The Helixor method had been to revolve a cylinder with water in it, thus creating a vortex. In the mixing process, the winter mistletoe juice was put in the cylinder and the summer juice dropped into the vortex. Now the mixing process takes place in a vessel in the form of an egg-shaped path-curve surface—in other words, in a 'counterspace'.

Not only in the field of medicine did Rudolf Steiner respond to questions concerning a revitalizing of scientific thinking, but also in the field of agriculture. Here, too, Steiner gave answers from this new science of the living world. For instance, he gave exact indications for ways of making preparations to be used on fields and woods and in making compost.

Here again it is a question of creating 'inner spaces' out of organic materials, such as cow-horns, sheep skulls, stag's bladders, animal intestines and the like. Until tried out, as today on farms all over the world, such indications seemed very far-fetched. Nevertheless, small quantities of substance put into such sheaths and exposed to the seasonal influences mature into fertile materials, which, when applied as it were homoeopathically, do bring forth most surprising results.

Chapter 4
From Archimedes to the Copernican Revolution[1]

It is not easy to understand why the field of research into a science based on the mathematical conceptions we have here been at pains to describe takes so long to become more universally accepted.

Every day one experiences quite practically the difference between the force of gravity and those forces by means of which one stands upright on the earth and walks over its surface. Surely, there is a difference between these two experiences!

It is true that a relatively small number of people have had the opportunity of experiencing Eurythmy or Bothmer Gymnastics[2] and few have made a thorough study of these new mathematical conceptions. Moreover, a one-sidedly materialistic education has clearly had a profound influence on the way people think today.

The most obvious reason for this discrepancy is surely the emphasis on analytical methods in education generally, and especially in scientific training. We are surrounded by a technology based on algebraic formulae, where the picture-making activity has been reduced to symbolism. Furthermore, the predominance of very physicalized sports clearly has its effects, in real life and also through the media.

In recent decades, there is a greater and greater awareness of the effects of modern life on younger generations and questions such as prison sentences and even capital punishment loom large. Unprecedented behaviour and the small wars which break out in various parts of the world reveal only too often the ugly head of nationalism, and also worldwide economic problems. The involvement of competitive sports with economics and the idea of buying and selling human beings is surely itself inhuman.

In face of all this, to some it may well seem abstract to put so much emphasis on what may appear to be merely intellectual studies. The fact is, however, that we can only see what we are able to think, and it is certainly possible to find a balance in clear thinking through such studies. Above all, such work must more and more become an integral part of modern education.

Our task here has been to understand the qualities in addition and multiplication and the significance of such processes as analysis and synthesis, and above all to find a balance. Mathematics, itself an art as well as a science, has a powerful influence, both for good and for ill, on individuals and therefore also on historical development.

In this connection it is fascinating and very instructive to compare two fundamental and quite elementary mathematical curves: the spiral of Archimedes and the logarithmic spiral. The first rests on the law of addition—the constancy of equal steps—and the second on the law of multiplication. In the latter it is the *proportion* expressed by any *two adjacent steps* which remains constant throughout the curve (cf., step measure and growth measure (p. 22ff), and Figs 6 and 7 (p. 25)).

The Archimedian spiral rests on concepts pertaining to physics and mechanics and will be found only in the inorganic world, whereas the logarithmic spiral comes to expression in living phenomena. All spirals in plants, shells and other living forms are logarithmic. In comparing the one kind of spiral with the other we move, as it were, from ancient Greece and pre-Christian times to the Renaissance and the time of the Reformation.

The Archimedian spiral in Cartesian space

Draw a set of concentric circles outward from a fixed point, making them grow in equal steps, and insert a set of equiangular radii from the centre. The pattern forms the matrix for a family of Archimedian spirals, originating in the central point and leading outward. In Euclidean geometry these curves are finite; in modern geometry each curve may be thought of as leading out to a point at infinity on the line at infinity of the plane.

The simple picture of circles or spheres growing larger, expanding outward from a central point in arithmetical progression or step measure, brings to mind the idea of a geocentric universe. It accords with our natural, everyday experience of being at home in our own physical body, from which we look out into the surrounding distances of space.

The ancient Mysteries, such as those of Egypt, Greece and Hibernia, accompanied the descent of humanity to the more earthly civilizations of recent time. The triple spiral at the entrance to the underground passage in the tumulus at New Grange in Ireland is a beautiful example of the Archimedian

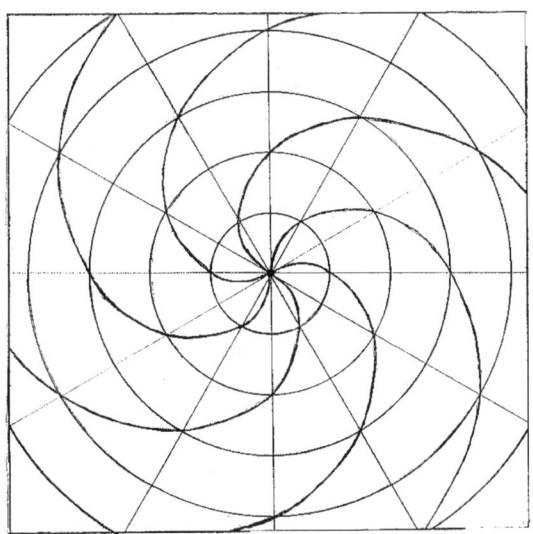

Fig. 17 *Archimedian spirals on circles in step measure*

Fig. 18   *Greek frieze showing step measure (end of 6th century BC)*

type of spiral. The Greek frieze in Fig. 18 shows the principle of the Archimedian spiral set in a repetitive step measure, which would not be possible in the case of a logarithmic spiral.

Although the Pythagoreans had discovered 'irrational numbers', and by about 400 BC Eudoxus of Cuidos had investigated the subject of mathematical proportions and even reached the understanding of the Golden Ratio,[3] which later permeated art and also architecture, nevertheless Greek geometry holds to a point-centred and finite way of thinking about forms. This led ultimately to the Cartesian conception of three-dimensional space in the 16th century.

Among the great Greek philosophers, Archimedes (287–212 BC), who probably worked in the Alexandrian School, is famous as an originator of physical mechanics. The story of his discovery in the bath is legendary. He noticed that the amount of water overflowing from the bath-tub as he entered it was equal to the amount of his body in its process of immersion. Jumping out of the bath, as the story goes, he rushed naked through the streets, shouting 'Eureca!' (I have found it!). He had found the answer to King Heiron's question, as to whether the gold crown he had asked the goldsmith to make was in fact made of the pure gold he had given him, or whether it had been adulterated with silver. Archimedes' solution involved the gravitational law concerning weights and measures, in relation to the law of buoyancy inherent in water. (How interesting to think that the clue was given through the experience with water, rather than with earth!)

Another basic law of physics discovered by Archimedes is the law of the lever. The king asked how great a weight could be moved by how small a force. It is said that Archimedes demonstrated this with the use of a series of pulleys, and that he said: 'Give me a place to stand on and I will move the earth,' thus describing how effectively the lever works against the force of gravity. A physical law causes a physical weight to rise upward, thus overcoming the downward pull of the earth's gravitational force.

Clearly, the mathematical picture of the Archimedian spiral, well centred in a point, inspires the idea of a geocentric universe, although the Greeks did not yet think clearly in terms of three-dimensional Cartesian space.

Nevertheless, the Greeks came very near to changing the conception of the geocentric universe. Aristarchus of Samos (310–230 BC) put forward the idea that the planets move round the sun, but that the sun itself moved round the earth. Aristotle (384–323 BC) thought that the universe was a sphere, with the finite earth fixed at the centre; he did not accept that it moved. He was, however, in no doubt that the earth is spherical, observing the way a ship disappears over the horizon, indicating the curvature of the earth. He observed that objects fall downward and that water continually seeks a lower level, and he taught that the natural tendency of earthy materials is towards the centre of the earth. He saw, however, that the watery and airy elements surround the earth in layers, and considered that above them is a warmth sphere; flames burn upward, he thought, because they seek their natural home.

Aristotle, in those early times, not only contributed to the understanding of gravity and of motion, but he was a biologist and studied life in the beehive, in plants, animals, and even embryology. He even carried out dissections in his search for what it is that makes a living creature alive, as distinct from an inanimate object. He thought that all living creatures had what he called a nutritive soul, which guided their intake of food, that animals had also a sentient soul, so that they could feel, and that man has a rational, thinking soul. Aristotle laid the foundations for what was to come in science many centuries later.

The idea of a geocentric universe did actually continue into the time of the great discoveries, which established the idea that the earth is spherical. As late as in 1539 there appeared in *Cosmographia*, a main scientific journal of that time, the picture in Fig. 19, by one Peter Apian, who set the earth in the centre of a family of concentric circles in arithmetic progression.

Galileo Galilei, born in 1564 and famous for his astronomical observations with the telescope, also made his epochmaking discovery at this time in the Cathedral in Pisa. Watching a lamp swinging at the end of a long cord, he began to work out the law of the pendulum. This is a prime example of the growing interest in the laws of observed physical phenomena on the earth. Such thoughts led to the formulation of the law of gravity by Newton.

The time had come for the development of individual human thinking, the time—to use Rudolf Steiner's terminology—of the spiritual soul.

Our task here is to approach an understanding of the polarity between the laws of physics and those at work in organic phenomena, rather than enter into a study of the religious and philosophical arguments of this period.

Fig. 19 *The geocentric universe as depicted by Peter Apian in* Cosmographia *(1539). Step measure*

It is surely of significance that in the diagram of the system according to Copernicus (1473–1543), where he sets the sun in the centre of the universe, his concentric circles are not in step measure but in growth measure! Copernicus has moved from the measure basic to the Archimedian spiral to the growth measure of that type of spiral always found in living forms.

Copernicus and the spiral of life

In the diagram of the system of the universe according to Copernicus (Fig. 20), which appeared in *De Revolutionibus* only four years later than the diagram by Peter Apian, the sun appears in the centre of a family of circles which are not in the arithmetic measure characteristic of earth measurement. Copernicus's circles are in logarithmic sequence.

This is the time of the Copernican Revolution, born in the

Copernicus (1473–1543)

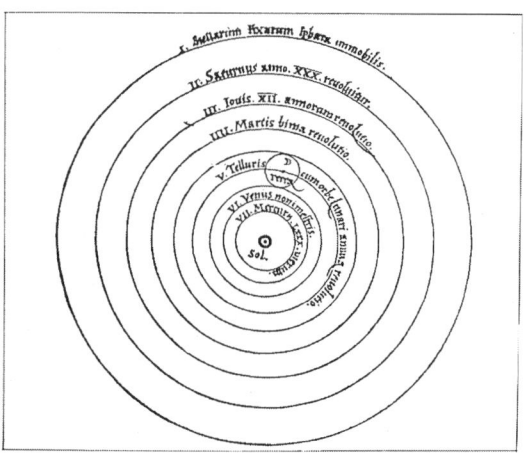

Fig. 20   *The heliocentric universe as depicted by Nicholas Copernicus (1473–1543) in* De Revolutionibus *(1543). Growth measure*

cradle of the Renaissance and the Reformation. Humanity strives onward in the attempt to understand the truths of existence. Individual thinking awakens with the birth of the spiritual soul, working in science, art and religion.

Figure 21 shows a set of interrelating squares and circles which accord surprisingly accurately with the measure expressed by the concentric circles as drawn by Copernicus (Fig. 20). This is the type of measure on which the logarithmic spirals in Fig. 22 are based.

Apian holds to the ancient idea of the earth as the centre of the universe; his sequence of circles set in step measure around a central point would form the basis of Archimedian spirals, as in Fig. 17. The circles drawn by Copernicus are not in this measure. He has drawn a family of circles in logarithmic sequence, around a point functioning as an innermost infinitude.

Copernicus puts the sun in the heart of what we have been calling a sun space; in Steiner's terminology it is a negative space, an 'ethereal space'. In mathematical terms, the sun is the 'Absolute' of ethereal space. This gives credence to the idea that the universe is a living organism.

In Fig. 21 the squares are basically tangential to the circles, indicating their cosmic quality (see Fig. 9[b]). The logarithmic spiral, in contrast to the spiral of Archimedes, appears in all forms of life; it is sometimes called the Spiral of Life.

There is harmony and balance in this way of viewing the Copernican picture. Surely Copernicus was aware of the difference between an ordinary point and a point functioning as an innermost infinitude—the Absolute of a living, ethereal space? It was the time when mathematicians were beginning to overcome the idea that three axes at right angles provided the only way of describing space mathematically.[4]

Nonetheless, science was on the way of descent into materialism, and the theory of Copernicus became the object of intense intellectual warfare at the time of the Inquisition, in which theologians and philosophers played a central part.

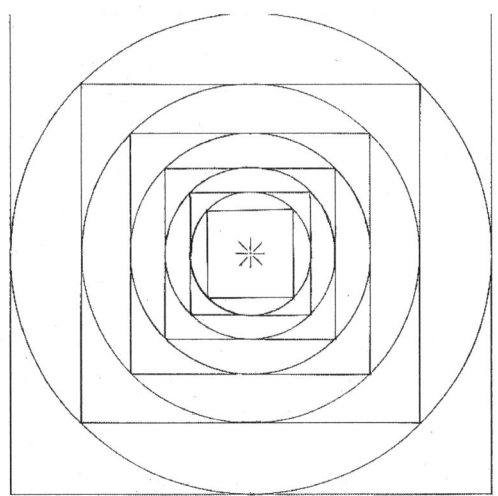

Fig. 21   *Confirmation of the growth measure in the family of circles by Copernicus*

Fig. 22   *Families of logarithmic spirals. Growth measure*

Indeed, Kepler (1571–1630) was himself a theologian, having first studied theology during the difficult time of the Reformation. Both Copernicus and Kepler were deeply religious Christians. Kepler, a Pythagorean and Platonist, still knew that a harmonious view of the universe must rest on a mathematical conception which neither falls into the pit of analytical thinking nor flies off into a visionary world of thought. Kepler's life was one of great inner and outer struggle, including excommunication by the Church; yet, in spite of all, he was able to achieve so much.

It will be helpful at this point to turn to what Rudolf Steiner said in the course of lectures given in Stuttgart in 1921 on the relation of the diverse branches of natural science to astronomy (Bibl. No. 323). In Lecture 15 he says: 'Whether we go by some ancient system or by the Copernican theories, in forming our pictured synthesis of the movements of heavenly bodies, we must relate the picture to man ... For a true science, we must accept that there is this relation.' Continuing, he says that the difficulties are formidable, inasmuch as we are restricted by the geometry of a rigid three-dimensional space.

In tine, we have to overcome space; we must transform it. If you are conscientious in your efforts to comprehend the phenomena, the idea of three-dimensional space will not suffice. You must envisage the interplay of two kinds of space. One of them, with the ordinary three dimensions, may be conceived as issuing radially from a central point. The other, which is all the time annulling the first, may not be thought of as issuing from a point at all. It must be thought of as issuing from the encompassing sphere—that is, the sphere whose surface is infinitely far away.

While in the former case the 'point' is of zero area, in the latter its area is that of a spherical surface of infinite dimensions. We must distinguish two kinds of point: a point of zero area, which it turns outward, and a point with the area of an infinite spherical surface, which it turns inward.

Geometrically it may suffice to conceive the notion of a point abstractly. In the realm of reality it will not. We shall not do justice to reality with the mere notion of an abstract point. In every instance we must ask whether the point we are conceiving has its curvature turned inward or outward; its field of influence will be according to this.

Difficulties there may be, but helped by the furthering work of George Adams, the difficulties are not so formidable. Take a look at the point in the centre of the family of Archimedian spirals (Fig. 17). That point in the centre is surely a point of zero area. It is the *nought* from which the outward steps proceed, as the circles (they could be spheres) grow bigger. This point of zero area, if it becomes active at all, will expand outward.

We may be helped to take hold of the idea of 'a point with the area of an infinite spherical surface, which it turns inward', if we contemplate Fig. 9(b), though this is more difficult. The tangent lines of the circles become the tangent planes of spheres.

From the plane-at-infinity, which is in fact none other than an infinitely large sphere, we may come inward in thought towards the innermost point. In so doing we retain the quality of the plane-at-infinity, and come inward with the spheres all clothed in tangent planes. This is a process which continues on and on inward, so that the innermost point has the quality of an infinitely small, spherical surface which turns inward.

This process is pictured in Figs 21 and 22 and in all the pictures of plant growing points; look especially at the developing buds in Plate 1 and at the beetroot in Fig. 2. Once our mathematical thinking has become sufficiently developed so that we 'see' the invisible innermost points and the invisible plane at infinity, we begin to see the invisible world of ethereal formative forces and to understand the 'negative space' which gives rise to the laws of living organisms.

Chapter 5
The Search for Meaning

The search for the meaning of life and a comprehension of its laws continues through the ages, at first through religion, also through art, and in our time especially by means of science and technology. It was Rudolf Steiner's great achievement to bring these three together in an absolutely modern sense, answering the questions of striving men and women.

The term 'spiritual science' means the spiritualizing of modern science, and the name 'anthroposophy' means wisdom concerning the human being. Both require the honest striving after truth through clear thinking. Knowledge today requires the raising of clear, intellectual thinking into what Rudolf Steiner calls Imagination, Inspiration and Intuition.

Another way of putting it would be to say that today we are free to find our own way to the truth, using our own thinking, feeling and willing to get beyond a one-sided materialistic view of the world.

It is instructive to insert here what might be called a time map of the lives of great people incarnated between the 15th and the 19th centuries.

Newton was born in the year that Galileo died. It was he who saw the apple fall from the tree and, pondering on it, reached the idea of universal gravitation and the law of inertia. Together with Leibnitz, Newton developed the powerful technique of the calculus, based on analytical mathematics, with the aid of algebra.

His method was in line with the intentions of René Descartes; he aimed to find a solution to the whole problem of planetary motion, and he thus extended the idea of earth space into the wide reaches of the universe.

It is with this way of thinking that astronomers today

Descartes
1596–1650

Desargues	Leibnitz	v. Staudt
1593–1662	1646–1716	1798–1867

Copernicus	Kepler	Newton	Poncelet	Haeckel
1473–1543	1571–1630	1642–1727	1788–1876	1834–1919

Dürer	Galileo	Pascal	Hegel	Cayley
1471–1528	1564–1642	1623–1662	1770–1830	1821–1895

Leonardo	Bacon	Rembrandt	Goethe	Darwin
1452–1519	1561–1626	1606–1669	1749–1832	1809–1882

- - - -/- - - - - - - - - -   /- - - - - - - - - - -   /- - - - - - - - - - -   /- - - - - - - - - -   /- - - - - - - - - -

15th C. 16th C. 17th C. 18th C. 19th C.

approach an understanding of sun and moon, the planets, stars and galaxies. It is, however, also such forms of thought which guide scientists in their search into the microscopic worlds of atoms, molecules, genes and so on. The extraordinary precision of modern mechanistic thinking leads to far-reaching questions in both directions of research.

Newton and Descartes both directly influenced the materialistic direction of science; Descartes made a very conscious decision to follow the analytical path, leaving his friend Girard Desargues to begin the development of modern projective geometry.[1] Kepler, a deeply religious man, who suffered excommunication from the Church, was one of the first to approach mathematically the idea of infinitely distant points.

Desargues was the teacher of Blaise Pascal and he was the first to bring the infinitely distant elements into geometry in a clear and explicit way. He is very little known, even today.

Leonardo da Vinci and the idea of ethereal space

While the scientists and mathematicians were attempting new ways of thinking, great artists were leading the way. Leonardo

and Dürer revealed so eloquently the laws of perspective, and
above all Rembrandt showed his knowledge of the innermost,
sunlike spaces. This wisdom is not only to be seen in paintings,
but it became enshrined in ancient buildings, even as early as
in the 12th and 13th centuries, when the great cathedrals were
built in Europe.

For what follows, I am indebted to two beautiful books that
recently came to hand; they are *Leonardo da Vinci's Abendmahl* by Hanns Feddersen,[2] and *Rose Windows* by Painten
Cowen.[3] In both books there are illustrations that spring to
life in the light of the mathematical ideas we have here been
contemplating.

Feddersen illustrates the foundation pattern of the Villa
Rotunda in Venice (Fig. 23). If continued inward, the inter-
woven pattern of squares and circles would lead to what we
have called an innermost point at infinity—a centre of ethereal
space. Feddersen then relates this pattern to Leonardo da
Vinci's painting of *The Last Supper*, as, for instance, in Fig. 24.

In Hanns Feddersen's mind, a square is a picture of earthly
measure, while a circle depicts a cosmic element. He quotes
Rudolf Steiner as follows:

Everything which an inhabitant of Mars would see, if he
could descend to the earth, he would perhaps find interesting to a greater or lesser degree, even if he did not fully
understand it. If, however, he were to see Leonardo da
Vinci's painting of *The Last Supper*, he would ... learn to
know of something from which he would recognize the
meaning of the earth.

Hanns Feddersen's own closing words are:

The secret of the painting of *The Last Supper* lies in the
interpretation of circles and squares—of the cosmic and the
earthly. As we eliminate the lines, which have been drawn
into the picture, we see them light up again in spirit. If we
have been thinking them in the spirit of Leonardo, then we

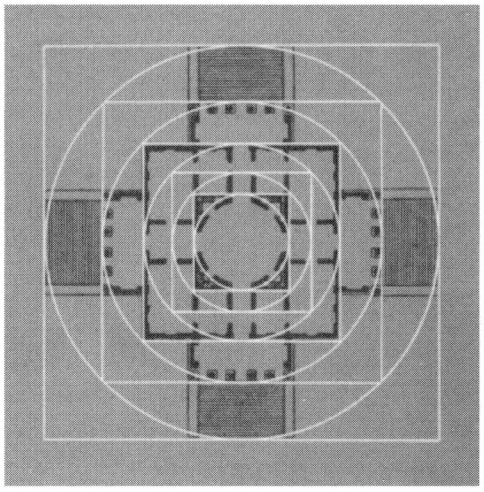

Fig. 23 *Foundation pattern of the Villa Rotunda, Venice*

Fig. 24 *Hanns Feddersen's perception of Leonardo da Vinci's* The Last Supper

know that we have been dealing with an invisible figure in which a deep truth is expressed. Through the circle, the Spirit of the Universe permeates the depths of earth, whose laws come to expression in the square. But it is in the interpretation of earth and heaven that the meaning of *The Last Supper* is clothed.

Looking at this picture with our mathematical studies in mind, we see the table like the plane of earth, upon which the cosmic-earthly events are taking place. The secret of the joining of the two realms is clearly revealed: the Christ takes the place at the focal point of a Sun Space—an ethereal space—on the earth. ('Where two or three are gathered together in my name, there am I in their midst.')

The timelessness of truth

Our study of physical and ethereal spaces is concerned indeed with a timeless truth, which must be kept alive and allowed to grow. The art of the great Gothic cathedrals lasted like a gleam of sunshine in those two early centuries, and still they stand there as witnesses of this truth.

Painten Cowen, at the end of his book, inserted several geometrical designs, relating them to the rose windows of a number of famous cathedrals and revealing clearly both the principle of the logarithmic spiral and the tangential aspect of the circle. Two of these diagrams are reproduced in Figs 25 and 26.

The mandala is, of course, also always a picture of a happening taking place beyond the realm of earth. The picture in Fig. 27 is also from the 12th or the 13th century; it is to be seen in the Trento Dom in Italy. This picture is remarkable in that it shows the Christ hanging on the Cross of the three dimensions, and yet at the same time He is using His sustaining, upward-moving, living forces to hold the weight of the Body as it hangs on the Cross.

Fig. 25 *Logarithmic formation in a rose window (12th–13th century) according to Painten Cowen*

Fig. 26 *The tangential aspect of circles in a rose window*

Fig. 27 *Mandala in the Cathedral of Trento (12th–13th century)*

The anti-gravitational, creative forces of the light create and uphold matter as it develops in living organisms. The truth speaks from times long past:

In the beginning God created the heavens and the earth. The earth was a vast waste, darkness covered the deep, and the spirit of God hovered over the surface of the water. God said: 'Let there be light', and there was light. And God saw the light was good, and he separated light from darkness. He called the light day and the darkness night. So evening came, and morning came; it was the first day.[4]

To close this chapter, in which the fundamental laws of the Archimedian spiral and those of the spiral of life have played an important part, we may pose an interesting question.

The advanced techniques of modern science, reaching out into the universe, have found and revealed in great detail the many spiral nebulae so many light years away. New stars and even planets have been found. More recent discoveries are the 'black holes', about which the theories are ever-changing. Is there life out there?

Investigation of the spirals pictured in Fig. 28 will lead us to the conclusion that they do not accord with the type of spiral typical of the Archimedian screw but with the equiangular or logarithmic spiral! They may well be based on the Golden Ratio, a measure belonging to the spirals in plants and much used by the artists of the Renaissance.

In the light of these considerations we may well believe the words which say that God created the heavens and the earth.

Fig. 28   *Logarithmic spirals in a spiral nebula*

Chapter 6
The Threefold Human Being

An urgent educational task

Rudolf Steiner began to speak and write about his conception of the threefold human being in 1917. In a small book entitled *Riddles of the Soul*[1] he placed on record, as he himself puts it, the result of 30 years of spiritual investigation.

The first translation of this book into English was made by George Adams, but it was out of print for 40 years before being brought out again by Owen Barfield in the form of selected essays entitled *The Case for Anthroposophy*.[2]

The understanding of this teaching concerning the threefold human being is greatly helped by a grasp of the laws of physical and ethereal spaces, and earthly and cosmic forces. Moreover, an understanding of the polar reciprocal nature of these polarities sheds much light on this whole question.

The realms of head, rhythmic system, and metabolic, reproductive, limb system, though clearly distinguishable from one another, nevertheless form a whole. This whole—the physical body—lives on the earth, between birth and death, in changing forms, with the capacities of thinking, feeling and willing, which also change as life proceeds.

Rudolf Steiner describes the threefold nature of the human being from two opposite aspects; the idea of polarity is inherent in all his descriptions. In the lecture course to teachers entitled *Education as a Social Problem*[3] (1919), Steiner summarizes as follows:

> From various aspects I have drawn your attention to the fact that man as he confronts us is, first, a man of nerves and senses; popularly expressed he is a head-man. As a second

member we have ... that part in which the rhythmic processes take place, the chest-man; and thirdly, connected with the entire metabolism is the limb-man, metabolic man. What man is as an active being is externally brought to completion in the physical configuration of these three members of his whole organism.

Head-man, or nerve-sense man;
Chest-man, or rhythmical man;
Limb-man, or metabolic man.

This lecture course to teachers describes the three changes in the child's life—from 1 to 7, 7 to 14, and 14 to 21—and the way the child reacts, in the first period to imitation, in the second to authority, and in the third to the power of real love. This is summed up by Steiner as follows:

Upon this threefold educational basis must be erected what is to flourish for mankind's future. If we do not know that the physical body must be an imitator in the right way [1 to 7], we shall merely implant animal instincts in this body.

If we are not aware that between the seventh and fourteenth year the ether body passes through a special development that must be based on authority, there will develop in man merely a universal, cultural drowsiness, and the force needed for the [political] right's organism will not be present.

If from the fifteenth year onward we do not infuse all education in a sensible way with the power of love that is bound to the astral body, people will never be able to develop their astral bodies into independent beings. These things intertwine. Therefore I must say:

Proper imitation develops freedom;
Authority develops the right's life;
Brotherliness, love, develops the economic life.

It is important to realize that in the very early years of a child's life, when the will is predominantly active and the power of thinking as yet undeveloped, it is the capacity of imitating all that goes on around him that will be transformed into the development of freedom of thought in later life. What a responsibility is given to all who care for small children—to see to it that everything one does is worthy of imitation!

It was during the chaos at the end of the First World War that Rudolf Steiner attempted to introduce into government circles in Germany the idea of the Threefold Social Order, based on his conception of the threefold human being. It retains the principles of freedom, equality and fraternity, voiced already in the French Revolution. According to Steiner, freedom must prevail in the spiritual realm, equality in the legal sphere of human rights, and fraternity in the world of industry and commerce, where money prevails. Each forms a part in the whole of every human being's life.[4]

Rudolf Steiner was not understood at that time, but he said that such a social order would come about in time, because it is organically related to life itself. He was himself forced at that time to move his work away from Germany, but he created what is now a worldwide movement, the Anthroposophical Movement, with its centre at the Goetheanum in Dornach, Switzerland.

Steiner was very outspoken concerning the confusion caused by a lack of clarity between these realms, saying that natural science, together with the machine, threatens civilized humanity with terrible destruction. The danger will arise should astronomy on the one hand and chemistry on the other persist in seeing the whole world in terms of a physical structure, thus likening it to a machine.

These are the influences that have become especially strong since the middle of the 15th century and rob men of their humanity. If they were to continue thinking in the way they think about machine-like astronomy and about the industrialism in which they work, human spirits would become mechanized, human souls vegetized, sleepy, and human bodies animalized.

It would seem true to say today, as we near the end of the century, that science still has a long way to go. Nevertheless, in social life generally it is widely accepted that everyone has a right to his own thoughts and also that there must be equality in the legal realm of human rights.

The problems are most evident in the third realm, where a lack of true concern for others causes inequality with regard to worker's rights, sexual promiscuity, problems in education, even wars (often resulting from confused economic situations as well as spiritual and cultural intolerance). It becomes more and more urgent to realize that it is only in thinking that a human being is and can be free.

Polar reciprocation and the idea of threefold man

The threefold nature of the human being in terms of the nerve-sense system, the rhythmic system and the metabolic system is comparable to the threefold nature of the plant in terms of root, leaf and blossom[5] which inspires the picture of man like an inverted plant. The nervous system, reaching down from the brain into the rest of the body, is reminiscent of the branching roots, while the flower, blossoming in the sunlight, is a picture of the cosmic pole and as such compares with the human reproductive system.

This is one way of describing the threefold human body. But elsewhere Rudolf Steiner describes it the other way round, and this is most enlightening when compared with the mathematical law of polar reciprocation. As we stand upright, the heavy body weighs down and relates to the gravitational centre of the earth, while the head, poised above and surveying the surrounding scene, clearly plays the part of the cosmic, sunlike pole. Heart and lung always hold the balance between the two polar realms.

In Dornach (26 August 1918)[6] Rudolf Steiner said:

... because science—the general world-conception of our time—does not recognize the meaning of what is 'emptier than empty', it is locked in materialism. There is in the human being, if I may express it so, a place which is emptier than empty—not in its whole, but included in its parts. The whole human being—and I mean the physical human being—is a being which fills out a material space, but a particular member of this human nature ... has actually an aspect that is sunlike—is emptier than empty. This is—you may take it or leave it—the human head. And just because the human being is so organized that his head can always empty itself and in certain of its parts become emptier than empty, through this the head has the possibility of allowing the spirit to enter into it.

In a lecture course given in Dornach in 1920, entitled *The Boundaries of Natural Science*,[7] Steiner speaks of the 'latent mathematics' in the body of the young child, and its relationship to the inner faculty of perception in regard to balance. He says:

Consider how the child gradually gains control of itself, how it learns to stand and walk, how it finally is able to maintain its own balance ... And if one can attain a certain insight into what is happening there, one sees that there is at work in the sense of balance and the sense of movement nothing other than a 'living mathematizing' (*ein lebendiges Mathematisieren*) ... We thus see a kind of latent realm of mathematics active in man.

It is this 'latent realm of a living mathematizing', at work in the processes of a living body, which underlies the new art of Eurythmy, created by Rudolf Steiner for the children of the first Waldorf School. At that time he saw that, as the child grows, a form of gymnastic movement is necessary. Both Eurythmy and Bothmer Gymnastics are based on the clear perception of the laws of both etheric and physical bodies.

In the study of the plant, we have become acquainted with the phenomenon of the hollow 'sun space' at the growing-point, recognizing it to be an anti-gravitational centre into which the uplifting, etheric forces pour, inducing further upward growth (Figs 2 and 3, and Plate 1). We may now apply this idea to the morphology of the human form.

We walk the earth with equal steps, overcoming the downward pull of gravity. The bones of the limbs are surrounded by muscular flesh; the bone is centric and radial. Moving upward, the bones of the ribcage are flat, forming a space for the rhythmic beating of heart and lung. Poised above it all is the head, quiet and still, but with a free, circling movement.

The skull bones are opposite in form to the limb bones. Their peripheral, planar forms enclose an inner space. They hold the brain, origin of the nerve-sense system. Here is a 'sun space', as in growing-point and flower, capable of receiving the light of thought.

This way of perceiving the human form is surely polar opposite to the one which sees man as an inverted plant! Both are true, and together they relate to one another, forming a unity, similar to the relationships of point, line and plane— positive and negative—in the mathematical discipline of polar reciprocation.

Fig. 29 shows a perspective transformation of the growth measure pictured in Fig. 5. This measure now takes place between *two inner infinitudes*. The comparison between this transformed growth measure and the forms of the spinal cord gives much food for thought. It points to the fact that the human vertebral column is poised between two cosmic poles. *Indeed, both the head and the reproductive-limb system have a cosmic as well as an earthly aspect.*

The comparison of the formation of the bones of the human spine with the projective transformation of a growth measure

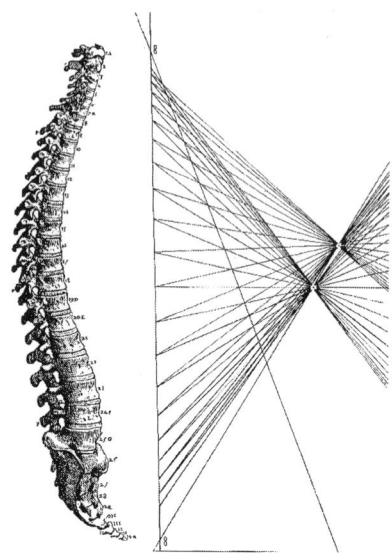

Fig. 29 *Perspective transformation of growth measure in the human spine*

functioning between two infinitudes appeared first in my book *Sun Space*.[8] It is a beautiful illustration of the rhythmical relationship between the poles of the threefold human form. We now see also the reciprocal nature of these two poles.

Our study of the forms of the human physical body has already shown that the head, origin of the nervous system, may be compared to the root of a plant, while the reproductive system compares with the flower and fruiting part of the plant. Now, however, it is the head which we are comparing to the sunlike, receptive system of the flower. The head may, indeed, become the receiver of thoughts, which are cosmic, ethereal forces.

Seen in the light of the mathematical conception of a sunlike ethereal space, the picture of the human brain, reproduced in Fig. 30, also contains much food for thought. It relates indeed to our morphological study, and is included here in order to suggest further research.

The picture relates to an article in the *Scientific American* of November 1989 describing the choroid plexus serving as a 'kidney' for the brain. It bathes the delicate cells in chemically stable fluid and plays a great part in protecting the whole nervous system.[9]

Look at this picture in the light of the thoughts which have led to the understanding of a sunlike, ethereal space. The outer bony surface of the skull encloses layer after layer, surrounding an innermost, empty space. Surely, this is a beautiful and true example of a 'sun space'.

We see what we think we see. Scientific research relies on clear, intellectual thinking. But thinking today can be activated beyond the perception of substance only, however rarefied. It is possible to cultivate an art of thinking that reaches beyond substance in the usual conception of space, and perceives the laws of the spiritual life which permeate us in thinking, feeling and willing.

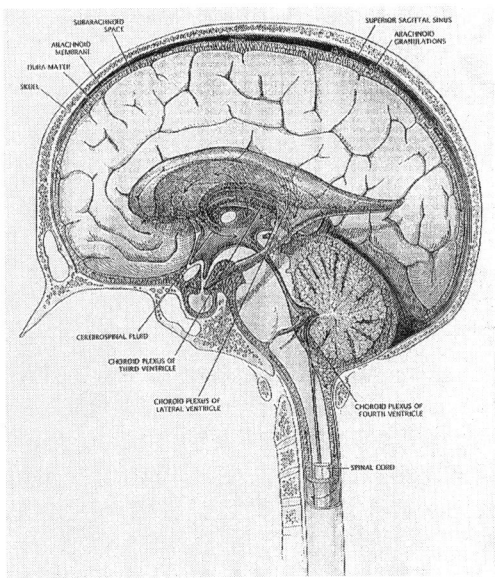

Fig. 30 *A modern scientist's picture of the human head*

Rudolf Steiner set himself this task and showed the way towards its achievement. For instance, in a lecture course in England in 1923 entitled *The Evolution of Consciousness*,[10] describing the first steps it is necessary to take in order to achieve higher knowledge, he said:

> All that is developed through the activity of thinking is a man's first supersensible member... First we have man's physical body that can be perceived by our ordinary sense-organs, and this offers resistance on meeting the ordinary organs of touch. Then we have our first supersensible member—we can call it the etheric body or the formative forces body... Here we have our first supersensible member, just as perceptible for a higher power of touching into which thinking has been changed as physical things are perceptible to the physical sense of touch. Thinking becomes a supersensible touching, and through this supersensible touching the etheric or formative forces can be, in the higher sense, both grasped and seen. This is the first real step into the supersensible world.

The intellect must become well schooled in our time—trained to understand and to use what is revealed to the wakeful senses, yet learning to reach beyond it. A one-sidedly intellectual thinking clearly leads to immense dangers, but also merely vague imaginings lead nowhere. A balance must be achieved, and this will come about to the extent that the idea of the threefold nature of the human being and of the whole universe is achieved.

Not only is the whole human being threefold in nature, but so also is the head in its entirety: on the one hand, the silent dome with eyes and ears relating to the surrounding world, and on the other the mobile, chattering jaws, with the rhythmic, breathing realm between them. Rudolf Steiner describes how the threefold body of one incarnation is transformed in the time between death and rebirth into the head of the following incarnation. Much depends on how we use thinking, feeling and willing while we are on earth.

This knowledge was there in ancient times, but as a teaching it had to become lost in order that the freely thinking human being might find it again on earth. The Christ came to help mankind, but in modern times it is we who must take the first steps from belief to knowledge.

In March 1925, a few weeks before he died, Rudolf Steiner wrote a letter to his friends in the Anthroposophical Movement, which he entitled 'Man in his Macrocosmic Being'.[11] It contains the following words:

The cosmos reveals itself to man, first of all, from the aspect of the earth and from the aspect of what is outside the earth, viz. the world of the stars.

Man feels himself related to the earth and its forces. Life gives him a very clear instruction regarding *this* relationship.

In the present age he does not feel himself related in the same way to the stars that are around him. But this lasts only so long as he is not conscious of his etheric body. To grasp the etheric body in imaginations means to develop a feeling that we belong to the world of the stars, just as we have this feeling regarding the earth through the consciousness of the physical body.

The forces which place the etheric body in the world come from the cosmos *around* the earth; those for the physical body radiate from the *centre* of the earth.

We have the opportunity, during our life on the earth, to recognize the truth of these words and to work towards an understanding of them. The 'living mathematizing' referred to by Steiner does indeed afford an essential bridge towards 'observing the invisible', leading towards the attainment of the three higher states of consciousness, which he calls Imagination, Inspiration and Intuition.

Like Rudolf Steiner, the great artists of the Renaissance were, as we have seen, very often scientists and artists at the same time. Two final illustrations (Plates 5 and 6), one from Renaissance times, the other modern, may conclude these studies.

The first (Plate 5) is Raphael's famous picture of Mother and Child. The two Beings are within the sun space of the cosmic circle. See Plate 5, Mother and Child within the circle. The second (Plate 6) is taken from a relief, a two-dimensional carving in wood by Emily Crockart, one of the early anthroposophical artists, who taught woodcarving in Rudolf Steiner House, London, in the early 1930s, between the two World Wars. She saw the little Child standing upright on the earthly dimensions of the wooden Cross, while at the same time standing in a sun space. He stands within the sun circle upon the Cross.

The task of crossing the bridge from earth to sun may perhaps be easier for the artist, yet cross it we must in science also today. The bridge is being created by individuals the world over. It is indispensable to education, to self-education and to the proper future development of science.[12]

Appendix 1
Christ and the Earth

From a lecture by Rudolf Steiner on
27 February 1910[1]

It is always said that Christ is constantly in our midst. 'I am with you every day until the end of the earth.' Now, however, man must learn to behold Christ and to believe that what he sees is real. This will happen in the near future; already in this century and in the following two thousand years more and more people will experience it. How will this actually occur? We might ask, for example, how we now see our planet. The earth is described mechanically, chemically and physically by science, according to the Kant-Laplace theory and the like. Yet we are now approaching a reversal in these fields. A conception will arise that will see the earth not in terms of purely mineral forces, but in terms of plant or what could be called etheric forces. The plant directs its root towards the earth's centre, and its upper part stands in relation to the sun. These latter are the forces that make the earth what it is; gravity is only secondary. The plants preceded minerals, just as coal was once plant life; this will soon be discovered. Plants give the planet its form, and they then give off the substance from which its mineral foundation originates. The beginnings of this idea were given through Goethe in his plant morphology, but he was not understood. One will gradually begin to see the etheric—the ethereal—because it is that which is characteristic of the plant realm. When man is able to perceive the growth forces of the plant kingdom, he will be released from the forces that now hinder him from beholding the Christ. Spiritual science should be an aid to this, but this will be impossible as long as man believes that the ascent of the physical into the ethereal has nothing to do with his inner being. It is of no matter in the laboratory whether a man has a strong or a weak moral character. This is not the case, however, when one is concerned with ethereal forces. Then one's moral constitution affects one's results. For this reason, it would be impossible for modern man to develop this ability if he were to remain as he is. The laboratory table must first become an altar, just as it was for Goethe, who, as a child, kindled his small altar of nature-products in the rays of the rising sun.

This will happen before long. Those who are able to say, 'Not I, but Christ in me,' will be able to work with the plant forces in the same way as that in which the mineral forces are now understood. Man's inner being and his outer surrounding work into one another reciprocally; what is outside transforms itself for us, depending on whether our vision is clear or clouded. Even in this century, and increasingly throughout the next 2,500 years, human beings will be able to behold the Christ in his ethereal form. They will also be able to see, however, that inner goodness works differently on the environment from the way evil works.'

Appendix 2
Christ and the Earth
by George Adams Kaufmann

*An Introduction to a course of lectures given in
London at the Rudolf Steiner Hall during the
autumn of 1927*

The present is a critical moment in our history. Men of all
shades of belief—religious, scientific, political—feel that this is
so. It is a crisis largely of knowledge and of fundamental
outlook. For the first time in the world's history, man is faced
with the task of building up a social life and civilization out of
his own conscious resources. All past civilizations were built
on a foundation of revealed religion or of 'higher knowledge'.
We may regard the revelations as coming really from a higher
source, as the believers do; or we may think them the mere
fanciful projections of instincts, fears, desires, unavowed and
unformulated in the unconscious depths of the soul. It matters
not; in either case, men were founding their lives on the
acceptation of what lay beyond their ken. Their ultimate
authority was not the freely guided, conscious intelligence of
man, but something beyond the limits of earthly human
consciousness—whether we aver with the believers that it
came from heights of God, or with the unbelievers that it arose
from hidden depths of nature. It was so for religious creed and
general world-outlook, and it was so also for the ordering of
social life.

In our time every man has the ideal of freedom—freedom at
least of mind and spirit. As to religion, many are still believers;
others are critics, sceptics, unbelievers. Yet they who believe
rightly claim to believe out of their absolute freedom, not
because they are told to believe but because they hold it to be

rational. And they who criticise and disbelieve do so again out of their freedom. However much we disagree, in this we are at one: in our sincere desire for the truth of life we have a common platform. We differ in our imperfections of knowledge and insight. Never was controversy more polite and tolerant; where it is not so, unlike our forefathers we glory not in our invective, but count it a reproach. The freedom of the spirit outweighs the passionate loyalties of the soul.

This fundamental urge of the times to spiritual freedom gives the first place to science. Science is the most wide-awake, the most detached, the most unbiassed of human activities. Hence the upholders of religious faiths are ever seeking to relate themselves to it; avowedly or unavowedly, they stand at the bar of science. They would fain have a religion tenable before the full critical consciousness of man.

This freedom of the spirit was hailed, at a religious conference not long ago, as the coming of a new phase in Christianity—the Christianity of the Holy Spirit.

But there is one great weakness in the tendency to subject religion to the scrutiny of science. The scientific intellect, though the most conscious, is not the deepest nor even the highest of man's faculties. Nor is it leading us, in the natural science of today, to understand more than a limited aspect of nature. It tends to show us nature in the guise of mechanism. It may be true, as is so often claimed, that to the physics of the 20th century the world is no longer material but spiritual. But the Spirit it reveals is that of a super-mathematician or technician, rather than of a Being filled with light and tenderness who would come near to the heart of a child.

Religion springs from a deeper source in our nature, which, in the present normal stage of our evolution is not yet lifted into waking consciousness. Critical intellect can at best grope its way in attempting to read the language wherein religious faith conveys its truths. These truths belong to a part of our being where we are still united, as nature-beings or as children of God, with the creative process of the world. It is the realm of intuition, inspiration, instinct.

The weakness above-mentioned shows itself in a widespread uncertainty of the religious life today. Much in the religious creed and practice of our time is tentative, experimental. Religion undergoes an atomizing process. Moreover, in the nature of the case, from the religious point of view, we are concerned less with the detailed laws and discoveries of science than with its wider theories and implications: the origin, age and ultimate fate of the earth; the nature of the material universe; the descent of man; the relation of mind and soul to the body. Now these are realms where science itself is largely speculative, often reaching far beyond the solid ground of its available facts, and therefore ephemeral in its conclusions. In the name of religion obeisance is done to one scientific tenet after another, only to find after a lapse of years or decades that scientists themselves abjure what they once swore by. This inconstancy of thought is damaging, and more so to religion than to science. Science has a right to change its ground, but our religious nature springs from an instinctive faith which craves for constancy.

In this position many people are feeling the need somehow to disclose resources of soul and spirit that lie deeper in us than intellect. Witness the widespread pursuit of psychology, psychoanalysis, psychical research. Eminent scientists and others are investigating with genius those hidden regions of the soul that are unborn to consciousness and, on the other hand, the strange powers and phenomena of human nature that are associated with abnormality, illness and death.

But there are those among us who would see farther. It can not suffice, we say, to turn the searchlight of intellect upon these deeper regions of the soul, teeming with the hidden forces of our bodily and spiritual nature. For even if we do so, we are revolving still in the same intellectual circle. The step for which mankind is ripe must be a further evolution of the soul itself, to become spiritually conscious in those regions of the soul where the deeper instincts and intuitions lie. Progress in science, and in religion too, will come by self-development—calling to life the higher faculties that lie hidden within us. This is not merely intellectual, but a spiritual, aesthetic and at once a moral task. Here the very method of discovery—demanding purity, unselfishness and reverence of soul—brings us very near to the heart of religion.

For all who perceive or dimly feel this need of the time, a mighty teacher has arisen in the first quarter of this century, in the individuality of Rudolf Steiner. Born in the early 1860s, he took this path of inner development most thoroughly, most rigorously from the very outset of his life, and discovered its fruits with an abundance which appears miraculous. Yet he declares again and again, these are but the fruits of a higher nature in us all. To raise to clear consciousness those hidden realms of the soul where are the springs of love and worship is to behold the spiritually creative regions of the world, where nature and the human spirit have their common source. So does the seer become not only the inspirer of fresh religious life but the discoverer of nature's secrets. The creatures stand arrayed before him; their soul-forces surge through his being, illumined each and all by his own clarity of spirit. He learns the secret of the Good Shepherd. He enters the Garden of Paradise, where the myriad creative forces of his life appear to him in the pure fragrant imaginations of the plant kingdom. A new scientist is born in him; it is the new Adam. With full clear consciousness he apprehends what the mystic has described out of his ecstasy: '... being renewed up into the image of God by Christ Jesus ... I say I was come up to the state of Adam, which he was in before he fell. The creation was opened to me, and it was showed me how all things had their names given them, according to their nature and virtue.'[1]

Rudolf Steiner became, out of his conscious seership, the pioneer of a new stage in science. First of all modern men, he revealed to us once more the *living* earth (known even as late as the 17th century to Kepler), while in the history and evolution of mankind he saw and renewed within himself the great truths of religion, and above all of Christianity. For in his spiritual vision he beheld once more the scenes of Palestine, and recognized the fundamental fact of Christianity: that Christ, in accomplishing the Mystery of Golgotha, became the very Spirit of the Earth, to live henceforth in and with humanity on earth. These things cannot be understood with a science which sees the forces of nature only in mechanical or numerical terms. To understand the Christian doctrines, we must first gain a science whose images are of a higher and more living kind. Such, for example, is the science of ethereal forces in nature that Rudolf Steiner and his pupils have developed.

The forces of nature—those, for example, through which the plant world year by year provides, out of the rhythmic interplay of earth and heaven, the nourishment for man and animal—are woven through and through with the spiritual forces of the Christ. Christianity will be renewed when natural science rises to this understanding. In a word, it is the Christening of science that is needed, rather than the pruning of Christianity to 'fit in' with modern science.

In the light of a spiritualized science, Christian tenets which the enlightened of the 19th and 20th centuries thought they must discard as superstitions, or water down to mere poetic symbols, are born again for modern consciousness. It is the Christianity of the Holy Spirit, differing from medieval or primitive Christianity not so much in its content as in the fact that its truths are held accessible to human knowledge. For one who has this spiritual science, his understanding of the Holy Communion, the mystery of Transubstantiation, is one in kind with his understanding of the concrete facts of nature—in agriculture, for example, and in the science of human life and health. *In feeling*, this was so already for the medieval folk and for the early Christians; it is so to this day, undoubtedly, for the simple peasantry of many lands and for isolated Christians everywhere, where intellectualism has not yet undermined it. But for the humanity of today it needs to become so in full consciousness of mind. Only then shall we have religion vitally at one with the heart of modern life and progress.

The subject of Christ and the earth therefore concerns the Christening of natural science, and withal, the resurrection of Christianity itself. This Christianity can no longer be an exclusive or a missionary religion in the narrower sense. The Christianity of the Holy Spirit—born as it is into clear conscious thought—will comprehend all the great religions. As Rudolf Steiner often said, the Christian of the future, imbued with spiritual science, will be able to meet the Buddhist on a common ground, if the latter too has spiritual science. Each will affirm the religious truths of the other. Christianity is indeed ultimately for all the world; yet it will spread not by exclusion or denial of the great religions but by their confirmation. This is esoteric Christianity, which sees the relation of Christ Himself to the spiritual leaders of mankind—Zarathustra, Hermes, Buddha...

This is an age when by sheer economic power a dominant civilization is able to spread itself over the whole world, imposing its forms of life on all other races—primitive and civilized alike. Such a thing has never happened in history before. Distances of time are annihilated; it is an ease of communication that puts the whole world on the quick. The English-speaking peoples occupy a central place in this world-process. In addition, they have preserved, more perhaps than any other nation of European culture, an instinctive feeling for the religious foundation of life—for the relating of this life on earth to cosmic principles and divine issues. They will yet have the task to bear into the world not only the material achievements but the higher spiritual knowledge born of western civilization. The material achievements by themselves, in reaction with the archaic cultures and traditions of the East, are fraught with peril. That is a familiar fact today. But the onward march of the free and objective spirit to which the real greatness of science is due will bring us into the realms of 'spiritual science', and the spread of this will be world-healing and world-union.

We return to what was said at the beginning. Modern civilization makes the gigantic effort to base all forms of life on human freedom, human consciousness. Well-nigh insuperable difficulties of the age arise out of this fact. Mankind today stands at a fine point of balance. This freedom involves polarity: the noblest heights of realization are before us; yet on the side of arrogance we see the depths of materialistic anarchy and bondage. However man may claim the freedom of his spirit, he owes his existence to the divine beings who created him and it was they who made him free. The freedom of man is a divine, not a mere human issue; for from the beginning it involves the destinies of the divine beings. Clear spiritual insight shows us that for the realization of his freedom man must find his union with Christ. Here is the mystic point where the true dignity of man, his highest stature, joins with simplicity, humility and reverence. Christ is the Being who with the 'Spirit of Truth' enables man to realize his freedom. Therefore the social civilization which we seek must stand— nay, must be edified from the beginning—in the sign of Christ. This is the conscious or unconscious striving of all who are imbued with the humane and cosmopolitan spirit of the age, seeking for amity between the nations and for the changing of industrial chaos into economic brotherhood. Christ as the Spirit of the Earth is their quest.

Rudolf Steiner—teacher of modern humanity on a truly cosmopolitan scale—is no longer with us. He died with the first quarter of this century—but not before he had laid the foundations for a world-movement that can bring regeneration to all departments of life. The present course of lectures will attempt to introduce a wider public to the spiritual science which he taught, showing how we find our way once more, by a true development of science, to the centre and focus of all life in Christ. The lectures will be based on Rudolf Steiner's written works, in which the foundations of Anthroposophy or modern spiritual science are developed, and, above all, on his hitherto unpublished lecture-cycles—notably those that deal with the Earth in its relation to the Heavens, with the history of the Creation, and with the four Gospels.[2]

Notes and References

Introduction

1   George Adams, 'Ancient and Modern Geometry in Physical and Ethereal Spaces', first printed privately in English by the author in *Space and the Light of the Creation*, London, 1933. In the same year there appeared an article under the same title in the magazine *Natura*, No. 5/6, Dornach, Switzerland, 1933. Adams was preparing a similar short introduction to the idea of physical and ethereal spaces and the etheric formative forces, when he died in 1963. These now exist in English, *Physical and Ethereal Spaces*, Rudolf Steiner Press, London, and in German, *Von dem aetherischen Raum*, Verlag Freies Geistesleben, Stuttgart.
    It was in 1916 that George Adams Kaufmann first heard of Rudolf Steiner and became a member of the Anthroposophical Society in London, devoting the rest of his life to the work.

2   Olive Whicher, *Sun Space*, Rudolf Steiner Press, London, 1989, and *Sonnenraum*, Philosophisch-Anthroposophischer Verlag am Goetheanum, Goetheanum, Dornach, Switzerland, 1989.

3   Rudolf Steiner, *Geheimwissenschaft*, Rudolf Steiner Verlag, Dornach, Switzerland. English translation by George and Mary Adams, *Occult Science*, Rudolf Steiner Press, London, 1979.

Chapter 1

1   Rudolf Steiner's autobiography, *The Course of my Life*, New York, 1988, Bibl. No. 28 in the German collected works.

2   For example, Dr Ita Wegman, Dr Elizabeth Vreede, Dr Ehrenfried Pfeiffer, Dr Ernst Lehrs, Dr Wilhelm Zeylans van Emmichoven, Dr and Frau Dr Rudolf Hauschka.

3 Rudolf Steiner and Ita Wegman, *Fundamentals of Therapy*, London, 1983. Bibl. No. 27. (New edition: *Extending Practical Medicine*, London, 1996.)

4 Günther Wachsmuth, *Erde und Mensch*, Dornach, 1980; Gerbert Grohmann, *Die Pflanze als Lichtsinnesorgan der Erde*, Stuttgart, 1962. (Neither is translated.)

5 Louis Locher-Ernst, 'Die Moderne Entwickelung der Geometrie und Goethe's Idee der Metamorphose', in *Goethe in unserer Zeit*, Dornach, 1949. (Untranslated.)

Chapter 2

1 George Adams, *Physical and Ethereal Spaces*; George Adams and Olive Whicher, *The Plant between Sun and Earth and the Science of Physical and Ethereal Spaces*, London, 1980.

2 See Note 2, Introduction.

3 See Note 1, Chapter 2.

4 See Chapter 1, pp. 11–12, and Reference Note 3.

5 See *The Plant between Sun and Earth*, by George Adams and Olive Whicher, London, 1980 (Stuttgart, 1979; Paris, 1982).

6 *The Plant between Sun and Earth*, Chapter VI, page 139.

Chapter 3

1 See Note 5, Chapter 2.

2 See Note 1, Chapter 2.

3 The upward-drawing force of life.

4 The plane-at-infinity of Earth-space.

5 Lawrence Edwards, *The Vortex of Life, Nature's Patterns in Space and Time*, Floris Books, 1993.

6 Georg Sonder: article in *Elemente der Naturwissenschaft*, No. 58, Dornach, 1993. (Not translated.)

Chapter 4

1 The formulation of this chapter owes a debt of gratitude to *The Cambridge Illustrated History of the World's Science* by Colin

A. Ronan, Cambridge University Press, Newnes Books, second edition 1984. In this are included Figs 19 and 20.

2 Fritz Graf von Bothmer, *Gymnastische Erziehung*, Stuttgart, 1981. English translation, *Gymnastic Education*, London, 1959.

3 The Golden Section is expressed geometrically by dividing a straight line into two parts such that the ratio of the smaller part to the larger equals the ratio of the larger part to the whole.

4 A study of Rudolf Steiner's lecture course Bibl. No. 201 is recommended here, entitled *Man, Hieroglyph of the Universe* (April/May 1920), London, 1972.

Chapter 5

1 Girard Desargues (1593–1662): see George Adams, *Strahlende Welgestaltung*, reprinted Dornach, 1965; Olive Whicher, *Projective Geometry*, second edition, London, 1971.

2 Hanns Feddersen, *Leonardo da Vinci's Abendmahl*, Urachhaus, Stuttgart, 1975.

3 Painten Cowen, *Rose Windows*, Chronicle Books, San Francisco, Prism Edition, 1979.

4 Genesis 1:1–5.

Chapter 6

1 Rudolf Steiner, *Von Seelenrätzeln, Riddles of the Soul.*

2 Owen Barfield, *The Case for Anthroposophy*, London, 1970.

3 Rudolf Steiner, *Die Erziehungsfrage als Soziale Frage*. English: *Education as a Social Problem*, Anthroposophic Press, New York, Bibl. No 296.

4 Rudolf Steiner, *The Threefold Social Order*, Anthroposophic Press, New York, 1966, and *Towards Social Renewal*, Rudolf Steiner Press, London, 1977.

5 See *The Plant between Sun and Earth* by George Adams and Olive Whicher, first published in 1952 by the Goethean Science Foundation, Clent, Stourbridge, Worcs, with a preface by Ehrenfried Pfeiffer. The second edition, revised and enlarged by

Olive Whicher, was published in German by Verlag Freies Geistesleben, Stuttgart, in 1979, in English by Rudolf Steiner Press, London, in 1980, and in French by Editions du Centre Triades, Paris, in 1980.

6 Rudolf Steiner, *Die Geheimnisse der Sonne und des drei-geteilten Menschen*, Bibl. No. 183, Dornach, August, 1918.

7 Rudolf Steiner, *Grenzen der Naturwissenschaft*, Bibl. No. 322, Dornach, September 1920. English: *The Boundaries of Natural Science*, with an introduction by Saul Bellow, Anthroposophic Press, New York, 1983.

8 See Note 2, Introduction.

9 The article in the November 1989 number of the *Scientific American* deals with some most interesting modern research. It is referred to here in order to encourage further research.

10 Rudolf Steiner, *Initiations-Erkenntnis*, Bibl. No. 227, Penmaenmawr, August, 1923. English: *The Evolution of Consciousness*, Rudolf Steiner Press, 1979.

11 Rudolf Steiner, *The Michael Mystery*, Rudolf Steiner Press, 1956

12 Recommended recent publication—Nick Thomas, *Entscheidungskampf im Atherischen*, Verlag am Goetheanum, Dornach, 1995. English edition: *Battle for the Etheric Realm*, Temple Lodge Publishing, London, 1995.

Appendix 1

1 Rudolf Steiner, *Das Ereignis der Christus-Erscheinung in der Atherischen Welt*, Bibl. No. 118. *The Reappearance of the Christ in the Etheric*, Anthroposophic Press.

Appendix 2

1 Journal of George Fox.

2 Rudolf Steiner's books and lecture cycles are now available in many languages worldwide.

A note of the cover picture,
The Archangel Michaël

He rides the Horse of the Intellect, arms outspread, holding a balance. Above is the winged Angel Realm of the Light of Thought, based on the Intellect, yet rising above it. Below is the Realm of the Dragon, held down by the Sword of Michaël; he controls, but never kills the Dragon. Darkness is a necessary part of the Whole. Both Light and Darkness play their part in creating the Rainbow, the colour-flooded Cup of Worlds.

It is the task of modern science, having achieved so much today, to strive further, towards a true understanding of the laws of living organisms in Universe, Earth and Man.

(Olive Whicher)

COLOUR PLATES

Magnified section of a young growing-point

Avenue at Middelharnis, by Hobbema

Adoration of the Shepherds, by Rembrandt

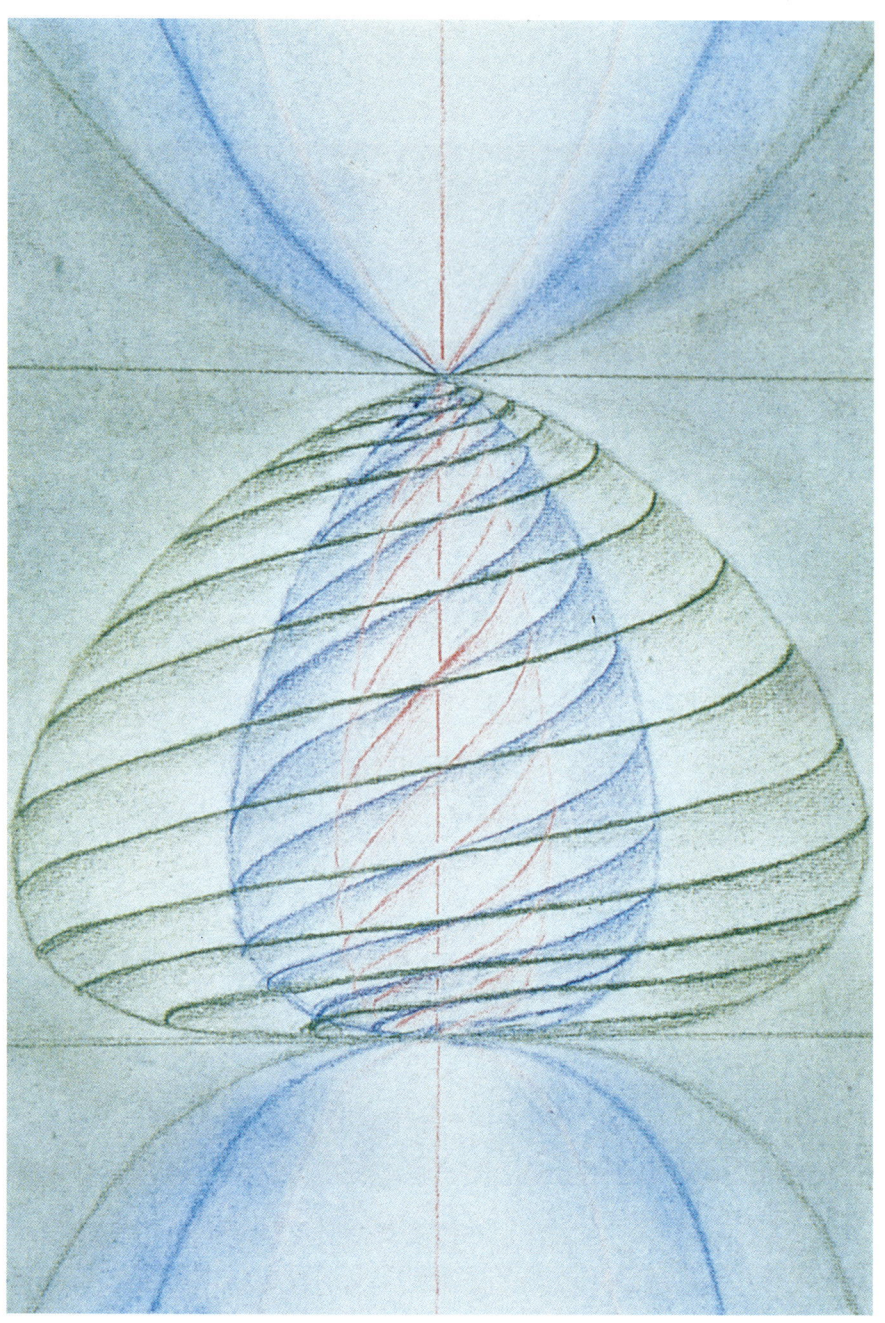

Path curve surfaces in ethereal space

Mother and Child within the circle by Raphael (1483–1520)

*Emily Crockart's woodcarving of the Child in a sun space standing on
the Cross (20th century)*